THE STARS OF FOOTBALL 2027

THE WORLD'S BEST PLAYERS

RODOLPHE GAUDIN

GELDING STREET PRESS

A Gelding Street Press book
An imprint of Rockpool Publishing

PO Box 252
Summer Hill
NSW 2130, Australia

geldingstreetpress.com
Follow us! geldingstreet_press

First published under ISBN: 9782036083660 as
Les Etoiles du Football © Larousse 2025

This edition published in 2026 by Rockpool Publishing
ISBN: 9781922662392

Cover photo credits: Shutterstock
Other photo credits listed on p. 200

Typeset by Ethan Cohen Stoddart
Adapted to English by Russ Gibbs
Adaptation edited by Lisa Macken

NATIONAL LIBRARY OF AUSTRALIA
A catalogue record for this book is available from the National Library of Australia

Printed and bound in China

10 9 8 7 6 5 4 3 2 1

BARÇA

CONTENTS

INTRODUCTION

The Stars of Football 2027 profiles more than 90 players and is packed full of stories about the biggest names from the top club leagues and the World Cup. In this new edition PSG players who dominated European football at home and abroad in 2025 and 2026 are well represented, and deservedly so! The team built by Luis Enrique is set to continue to shine in the coming seasons, and in the meantime world superstars Lamine Yamal, Erling Haaland, Mohamed Salah and Kylian Mbappé and their respective teams will chase down the Parisians. However, French fans were not dreaming: Paris Saint-Germain is now the team to beat on the continent. Paris is truly magical . . .

Luis Enrique succeeded in imposing his ideas and became a respected coach, one who is not questioned, and a young and ambitious group was born. With Dembélé as the leader, Doué a divine surprise, Vitinha a midfield metronome and Marquinhos the perfect captain, Paris marched on Europe. Liverpool, Arsenal, Inter Milan: so many battles won without wavering, the kind of conquest we'll talk about again and again. PSG asserted itself in style as a European powerhouse in response to 20 years of persistent schizophrenia.

Each year football introduces us to several players on the path to superstardom. In this book you will discover their unique journeys, the challenges they've overcome and the adversity they've faced to reach the top. *The Stars of Football 2027* is here to bring you closer to the most prominent names on the planet, as the rest seek to emulate PSG's golden run.

Rodolphe Gaudin

UNITED STATES

Tyler ADAMS

BORN: 14 February 1999,
Wappingers Falls, New York

HEIGHT: 1.75 m

POSITION: Midfielder

PROFESSIONAL CAREER:
New York Red Bulls II,
New York Red Bulls,
RB Leipzig,
Leeds United,
AFC Bournemouth

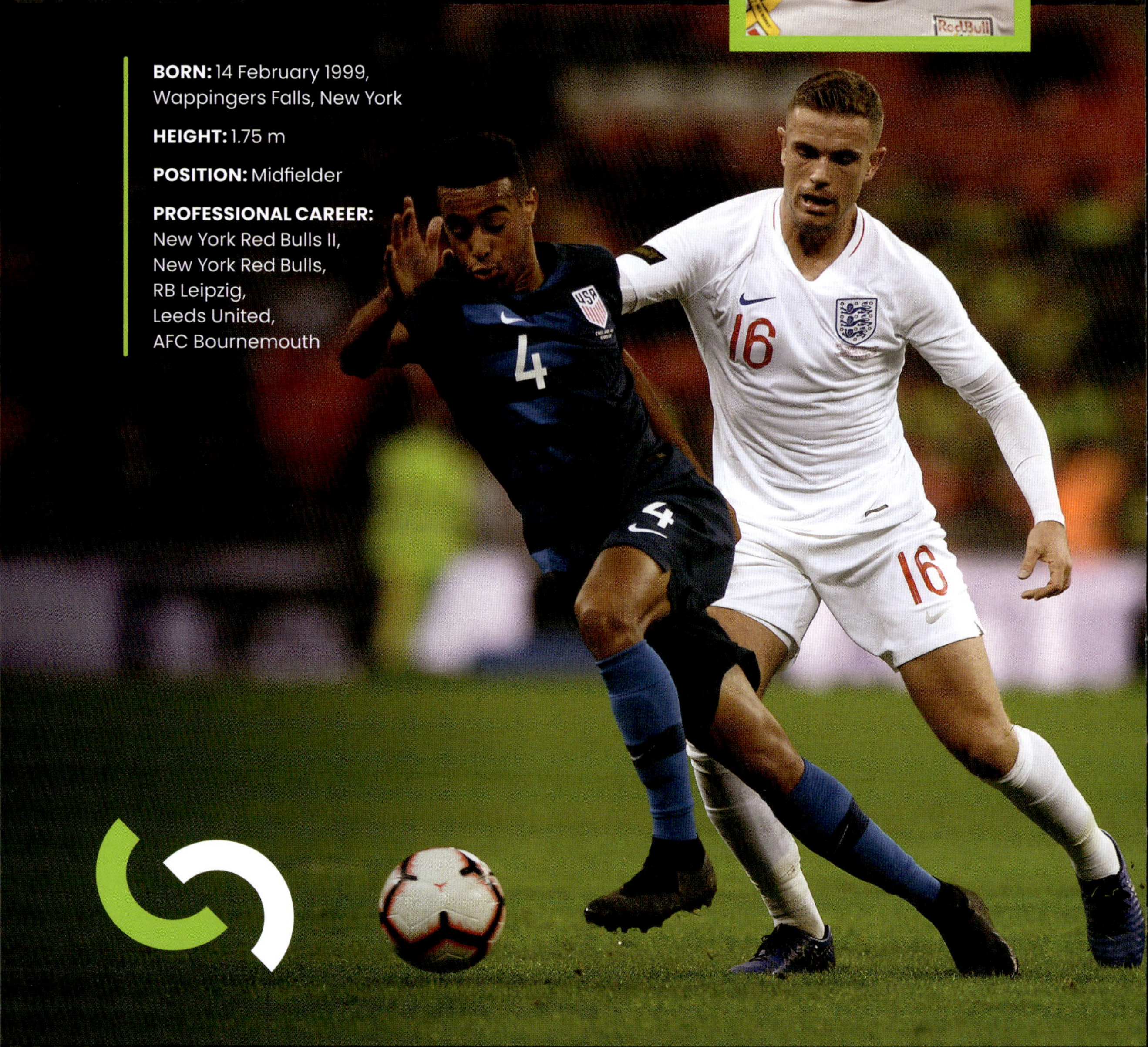

Aggressive, tenacious and disciplined: three words that have been applied to the playing style of talented United States midfield dynamo Tyler Adams and ones that he has made into the cornerstone of a career that is now flying high in the English Premier League. Versatility could be another. His ability to play either on the wing or in defence is an added string to an already impressive bow.

A product of his environment, Adams joined the New York Red Bulls Academy as a precocious youth, making his way through the U-13, U-14 and U-16 squads and into the reserve team. That side, the New York Red Bulls II, played their football in the United Soccer League and it proved to be the perfect stomping ground for young Adams to learn, enhance and hone his craft.

A season at that level led to a promotion into the MLS squad and a debut in 2015, scoring in a friendly fixture against Chelsea and going on to make his MLS debut in a fixture against the San Jose Earthquakes. With Adams cementing a first team place there were covetous eyes looking at his progress, and New York's sister club RB Leipzig managed to entice the midfielder away from the States.

Adams made his first start in the Bundesliga in 2019 against Fortuna Düsseldorf, going on to make more than 100 appearances in four seasons and scoring a pair of goals. One of those goals was the match winner against Atlético de Madrid in the quarter finals of the UEFA Champions League. His metronomic displays earned him a €20 million move to Premier League outfit Leeds United, but in his one season at Elland Road the club was relegated to the championship.

Taking advantage of that fact was AFC Bournemouth which, clearly impressed by Adams' qualities despite an injury that hampered his end-of-season run-in, snapped him up on a five-year contract ahead of the 2023/24 season. He has been influential in the Cherries' steady rise up the table as they seek qualification for European competition for the first time.

On the international stage Adams made waves throughout his movement up the United States age grades, finally pulling on the national team shirt at senior level in 2017 in a 1–1 draw with Portugal after having represented his country at U-15, U-17 and U-20 levels.

DID YOU KNOW?

Captains tend to be experienced and knowledgeable and have been around the tracks a bit, so it may have come as something of a surprise to many when in November 2022 Tyler Adams was named as the leader of the United States squad appearing at the 2022 FIFA World Cup in Qatar. This acknowledgement of his outstanding leadership skills made Adams the youngest captain at the Middle East tournament and the youngest to lead the USA since 1950!

SWITZERLAND

Manuel
AKANJI

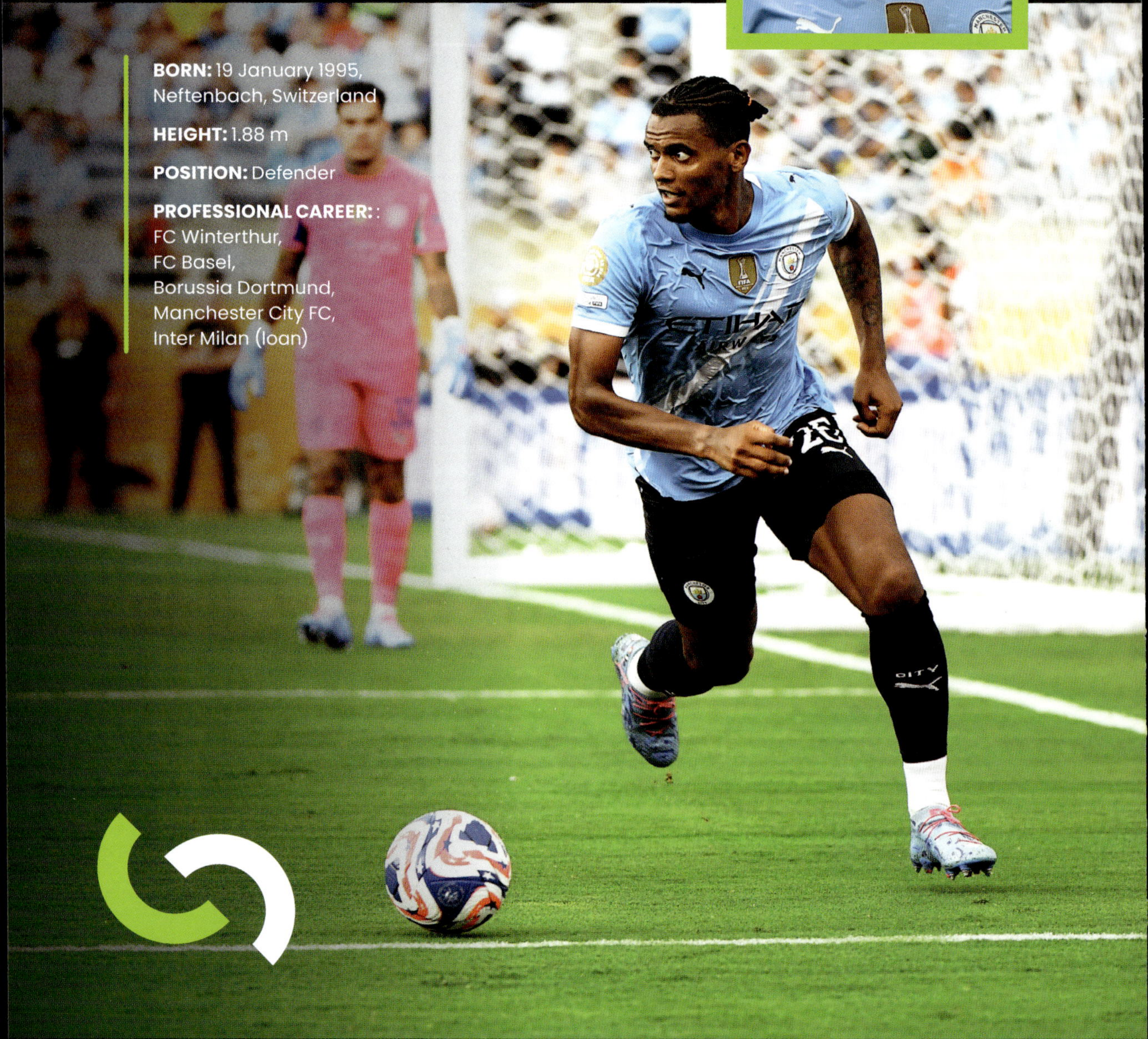

BORN: 19 January 1995, Neftenbach, Switzerland

HEIGHT: 1.88 m

POSITION: Defender

PROFESSIONAL CAREER: :
FC Winterthur,
FC Basel,
Borussia Dortmund,
Manchester City FC,
Inter Milan (loan)

You know what you are going to get with defensive titan Manuel Akanji. He has earned a reputation for always doing the right thing, at the right time and at the right tempo: 'My goal is that the opponent doesn't even get a chance to believe he can pass,' is Akanji's take on his all-action displays.

Born in 1995 in Neftenbach, Switzerland, Akanji grew up in a family where education and studies were valued as much as sports. He quickly distinguished himself by his discipline, and at school he liked his numbers and maths. 'Equations are like football,' he said. 'You have to understand before acting.'

Akanji applied this rigorous mindset from the very beginning, from the time of his debut at the small Swiss club FC Winterthur. He progressed without cutting corners and then joined FC Basel, where he discovered the requirements of the highest level. His reading of the game, his ability to defend standing up and his precise tackling quickly propelled him into the radar of the big European clubs, and in 2018 Borussia Dortmund recruited him. A defender who never panics, Akanji is fast but does not rush. He plays under pressure as though he has a second more than everyone else and, above all, he understands the schemes, instructions and moves. 'I've always been someone who wants to know why we do things and apply the same outlook to the field.'

In Dortmund, however, Akanji had his difficulties. The club's defence sometimes struggled to find stability and injuries hampered him, but for his part he did remain constant, and whenever he was selected the team was better. In the summer of 2022 Pep Guardiola saw in him what few had fully understood: a player of rare game intelligence. Manchester City wasted no time in signing him. At City Akanji quickly established himself. Versatile, he played in central defence, right back and sometimes even in midfield. Guardiola clearly adored him. 'He's a player who understands everything,' Pep said. 'You can explain to him an idea once and he applies it right away.'

The Swiss star participated in City's historic treble of 2023, playing in a series of big games but always remaining faithful to his philosophy: defend fairly without excess. 'I prefer it to be said that I make others better,' he revealed. 'That's my job.' That's what he does, game after game, with elegance and precision.

DID YOU KNOW?

Manuel Akanji has a surprising gift: he is passionate about mathematics and can solve many complex equations in a matter of seconds: a 2018 video in which he instantly calculated three-digit multiplications without hesitation went viral. Coming from a sporty family, with his mother being a former tennis player and his Nigerian father a former amateur footballer, the native of Neftenbach, a small village in the canton of Zurich, is also multilingual, speaking German, Italian, French and English!

AUSTRIA

David

ALABA

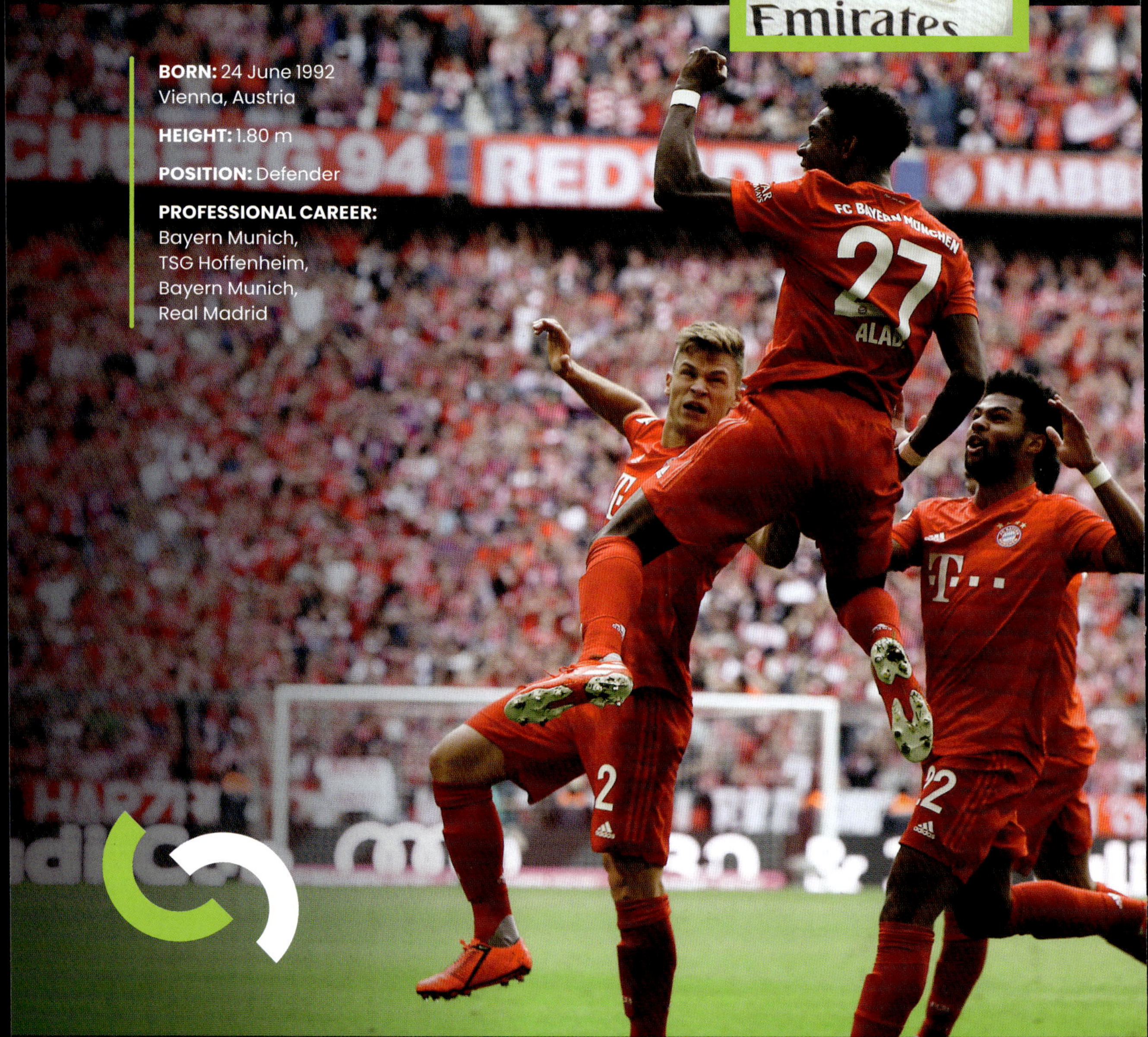

BORN: 24 June 1992
Vienna, Austria

HEIGHT: 1.80 m

POSITION: Defender

PROFESSIONAL CAREER:
Bayern Munich,
TSG Hoffenheim,
Bayern Munich,
Real Madrid

DID YOU KNOW?

When you are from Austria it is impossible not to be a ski fanatic. In the land of the kings of sliding, David Alaba is no exception. The left-sided player is a particular fan of Marcel Hirscher, several times champion of the downhill world. And when winter spreads its white coat over the Tyrolean peaks, David Alaba turns into an attentive spectator, especially in Kitzbühel, the temple of the sport.

Never in trouble as a youth, it was only when he was playing football that David Alaba refused to listen to authority. When his father George asked him to come home to the dinner table the little Alaba continued to play with his Viennese friends; otherwise, at school and in his everyday life the boy was a perfect role model.

The first black person to complete his military service in the Austrian army, George Alaba educated his children with the principles of respect. Unsurprisingly, David's father also sacrificed much for his son to succeed. As a youngster David was driven to and from training at Aspern SV by George, the father recovering in the family's old Ford Escort while David was learning the ropes on the pitch.

At the age of 13, David left the family nest for the Stronach Akademie, the training centre of Austria's Vienna. The following year he was spotted during a match in Tyrol by the famed Bayern Munich scout Werner Kern. Arriving in Munich, David initially found his integration tricky. The mentality at the German giant was hard to get used to, the Bavarian club arriving at tournaments spectacularly dressed in the official club tracksuit and in the most beautiful coach. Above all, Bayern always seemed to walk away with the trophy!

It was this culture of winning that Alaba learned over time, imposing himself on the team and earning a place in the first team as a rampaging left back, becoming known in the Rhine region as the 'complete footballer' – a nickname that was coined even before he was a regular in the dominant Bayern squad, then under the tutelage of Louis van Gaal.

Under the Dutch boss Alaba was a mainstay in the side for more than a decade, enjoying his time on the flank. With the talented French international Franck Ribéry placed in front of him, the duo became firm friends both on and off the field. In this Bayern juggernaut, Alaba won a multitude of prestigious titles.

In October 2009, at just 17 years and 3 months old, he became the youngest international in the history of Austrian football, making his debut in a 1–3 loss to France at the Stade de France in Paris. And he continues to write his success story, scooping the La Liga title and the Champions League in his first season at Real Madrid following his transfer from Bayern. Now that's what we call making your mark!

ENGLAND

Trent

ALEXANDER-ARNOLD

BORN: 7 October 1998
Liverpool, England

HEIGHT: 1.75 m

POSITION: Defender

PROFESSIONAL CAREER:
Liverpool FC

The blood that runs through the veins of Trent Alexander-Arnold is unquestionably a little redder than it is in most common mortals. This is because Alexander-Arnold, who is currently considered one of the best right-backs in the world, has been a loyal Red since he was six years old.

Very quickly, the young prodigy was spotted by Liverpool legend Steven Gerrard, who in his biography was effusive in his praise for a youngster who lit up the club's training base on a daily basis. In his book Gerrard wrote: 'Trent has a real chance of one day becoming a professional at a very high level, he has all the qualities for that.'

The Scouser was quick to prove himself worthy of the hopes of his illustrious elder. The lad, who once held Jamie Carragher's hand when he escorted the players as they entered the cathedral of Anfield, made his professional debut just days after blowing out the candles on his 18th birthday cake. It was October 2016 to be exact, and Tottenham Hotspur provided the opposition.

Much like the incredible turn of pace he showcased throughout his early displays, everything moved extremely quickly for Alexander-Arnold, and he capped his maiden appearance in the Union of European Football Associations (UEFA) Champions League in August 2017 with a special goal against the German side Hoffenheim. The following season he provided a record 12 assists in the Premier League, the most ever by a defender in the competition. A series of excellent performances saw him selected in the UEFA Best X.

Just a few months later, at 20 years old, he dethroned the Italian Christian Panucci to become the youngest player in history to play in two consecutive Champions League finals. These feats saw his reputation soar, the Golden Boy of the Reds being valued at a mind-boggling €100 million. This hasn't affected him, though, as the down-to-earth defender is seemingly impermeable to praise and has kept a cool head throughout, even retaining his shirt number of 66.

'We don't like to give them a little number in case they think they succeeded right away,' explained Lee Radcliffe, jersey management coordinator for Liverpool FC. 'For Trent, we chose this number because he was just coming out of the academy' – a number the star chose to retain despite his new status.

DID YOU KNOW?

Besides being an intelligent football player, Trent Alexander-Arnold is also passionate about chess. As a gift for his 20th birthday he met one of the absolute legends of the chessboard, Magnus Carlsen. The Englishman even allowed himself a small duel against the Norwegian, being swept away in 17 moves and five short minutes of play. As consolation he can always tell himself he outlasted Bill Gates, who was knocked out in just nine moves!

FRANCE

Bradley

BARCOLA

BORN: 2 September 2002, Villeurbanne, France

HEIGHT: 1.82 m

POSITION: Winger, forward

PROFESSIONAL CAREER: Lyon II, Lyon, Paris Saint-Germain

DID YOU KNOW?

On 14 February 2024, Valentine's Day, Bradley Barcola kissed his forearm to celebrate his Champions League goal against Real Sociedad, a game his team won 2–0. What did his gesture mean? In was a signal to his girlfriend, with whom he shares a tattoo that reads '4ever'. Love is beautiful!

On 16 May 2024 head coach Didier Deschamps announced the 25 players selected for the European Championship in Germany. The inclusion of the name Bradley Barcola came as no surprise, even though the youngster had yet to be called up to the senior international squad. However, his performances at club level could not be ignored by the Les Bleus manager.

'He has the ability to dazzle, to eliminate, to create through dribbling and speed,' Deschamps said of one of his prize assets. 'Bradley will become more effective with time.' The young Parisian's name had already been mentioned two months earlier, during the brace of warm-up matches against Germany and Chile, but Deschamps had left him on the sidelines. 'I felt that everything happened very quickly for him,' the coach said. 'He has confirmed since then he is ready.'

That famous Champions League quarter final against Barcelona became the detonator of the Parisian's awakening at the elite level. When he made his debut at the age of six with AS Buers Villeurbanne, little Bradley already had the potential to unhinge opposing defences. In 2010 he joined the Olympique Lyonnais academy, being selected all the way up to the U-18 squad. The top scorer at U-19 level with 11 goals in 17 games, he was quickly included in the team competing in the Youth League.

The date of 2 April 2023 marked a turning point in Barcola's career. At Parc des Princes he scored the only goal for Les Gones against PSG in a 1–0 victory. At the end of August he was transferred to Paris for five seasons. Naturally, when he turned up in his former backyard decked out in his new PSG colours the reception he received from the fans was frosty. Although he was booed by the supporters who had cheered him during his first match in a Paris shirt, Bradley Barcola played an active part in his new team's 4–1 triumph.

Three months later the French champions' new number 29 opened his goal account against FC Nantes in a 2–1 success with the team's head coach Luis Enrique full of praise for him. 'Bradley has shown since the start of the season that he's ready to play at the highest level,' Enrique said. 'He's just as valuable in provoking defenders as he is in the defensive rearguard.' Bradley soon became a key player for Paris, with his record at the end of the season for the capital club speaking for itself: the winger played a total of 39 games in his debut year.

BRAZIL

Alisson

BECKER

BORN: 2 October 1992
New Hamburg, Brazil

HEIGHT: 1.93 m

POSITION: Goalkeeper

PROFESSIONAL CAREER:
SC Internacional, AS Roma, Liverpool FC

He was the missing piece of the puzzle. In Kyiv on 26 May 2018, Liverpool lost 3–1 to Zinedine Zidane's Real Madrid in the UEFA Champions League final. For at least one of the goals scored by the Merengues, Reds' goalkeeper Loris Karius was held largely to blame. It thus became a priority for the club to recruit one of the best shot stoppers in the world, and two months later the English club took out its chequebook and signed Alisson Becker from the Eternal City: Rome. At a cost of €75 million the former AS Roma goalkeeper became the most expensive custodian in history.

What do you get for that price? A modern, complete goalkeeper who is half rock, half feline and always effective. For his first season in the Premier League Alisson made Reds fans very happy, going 20 matches without conceding a goal and more than one match in two with a clean sheet, which underlied his importance to the team. However, if there is one area where Alisson really impresses it's on his line.

DID YOU KNOW?

Transfer discussions between AS Roma and Liverpool over the signing of Alisson had been intense and everyone had heard about it – enough for almost namesake Alison Becker to have fun on social networks. 'Very excited to announce that I will be joining Liverpool as a goalkeeper,' the American actress tweeted. The day after, Liverpool confirmed the signing of their new goalkeeper.

Standing at 1.93 m tall, his impressive frame makes him excellent in the air, but he also has the agility and athleticism to get down to low shots. This combination, allied with some perfect positional sense, makes him the nemesis of opposition strikers. His uncanny reflexes from shots near and far are vital to the Liverpool cause. Just ask Lionel Messi and FC Barcelona!

Within 13 months the Catalan club had suffered two terrible defeats in the Champions League, nightmarish evenings that had one point of reference: Alisson Becker. Both times, in the second leg of the ties at the Stadio Olimpico and at Anfield respectively, Becker was an impassable wall who made all the difference. On two consecutive occasions he put an end to the Argentine number 10's dream of success in a fifth Champions League.

Goalkeeper for his international team since 2015, the Seleção number 1 really justified his huge fee in the final of the most important European competition, the Champions League. In the last quarter of an hour he pulled out two huge saves against Tottenham Hotspur, preserving Liverpool's lead. Madrid, on 1 June 2019, forever became Alisson Wonderland as Liverpool claimed their sixth cup with 'Big Ears'.

ENGLAND

Jude
BELLINGHAM

BORN: 29 June 2003

Stourbridge, England

HEIGHT: 1.86 m

POSITION: Midfielder

PROFESSIONAL CAREER:
Birmingham City, Borussia Dortmund, Real Madrid

DID YOU KNOW?

Jude Bellingham has worn the number 22 on his jersey for a long time, and he owes it to clever calculation. Due to his versatility he can play as a number 4, but also as a number 8 or a 10. Add it up and you get 22! It was his father Mark who had the idea, to better symbolise the multiple roles of his gifted son, always at ease in the heart of the game whatever his position.

The tearful farewell: in May 2023 Jude Bellingham found himself distraught, collapsed on the turf of Signal Iduna Park, Borussia Dortmund's cauldron of a home venue, inconsolable like everyone wearing yellow and black on that fateful day. While a ninth German championship title was within reach of the Schwarzgelben, the match scenario against Mainz for the last day of the Bundesliga turned into a nightmare. A 2–2 draw was not enough for Dortmund, who watched on as Bayern Munich stole the trophy out from under their noses with a last-minute winner in Cologne that saw the Bavarian giants retain their crown. For his last match in the Ruhr after three seasons, the young English midfielder obviously dreamed of an exit through the front door, garlanded and honoured. Apart from a German Cup, his time with the club remained empty of major titles. The film of his season must have paraded at high speed through his mind as the title slipped from his and his team's grasp.

It continued a season of enormous frustration for Bellingham, England having been beaten in the quarter finals of the 2022 FIFA World Cup by eventual runners-up France – this despite Bellingham being one of the stars of the entire tournament. On the stages of Al-Bayt in Al Khor Bellingham rose to the occasion, 'Jude Ball' releasing the full range of a complete player. He was a perfect bend of modern midfield dynamo, recovering the ball countless times, breaking opposition defensive lines with impunity and bringing danger to the opposition goal in and around the penalty box.

This prodigy from the West Midlands in the United Kingdom had been vaunted as a box-to-box expert and has had the power to intensify his game and direct those around him by actions alone. Naturally, these qualities of Jude Victor William Bellingham had caught the attention of a raft of clubs: PSG, Chelsea and Manchester City were all touted as destinations upon his Dortmund departure, but it was Los Blancos of Real Madrid that won the race.

For a long time English football lacked true creators, but now they have the perfect midfielder: he brings huge offensive ability but does not skimp on defensive effort, which makes him one of the most complete players in his position and for his age. Often compared to David Beckham, Jude Bellingham has a few years ahead of him to in turn achieve comparable status. His dynamic start to life in the Spanish Capital has only fuelled the feeling that this will be a case of when, not if.

FRANCE

Karim BENZEMA

BORN: 19 December 1987
Lyon, France

HEIGHT: 1.85 m

POSITION: Striker

PROFESSIONAL CAREER:
Olympique Lyonnais,
Real Madrid, Al-Ittihad

DID YOU KNOW?

Better than Thierry Henry! During the 2018–19 season Karim Benzema became the top French scorer in the Champions League, reaching the symbolic bar of 60 goals in the prestigious event. Overall, the Real Madrid striker has only three players left in front of him: Cristiano Ronaldo (121 goals), Lionel Messi (106) and Raúl (71). In December 2005 the native of Bron had scored his very first goal in C1 during a Lyon-Rosenborg fixture (2–1) played at Stade Gerland.

When he arrived at Real Madrid in the summer of 2009 just before his 22nd birthday, Karim Benzema entered another dimension. In the Lyon bubble the young striker was impressive and a standout star.

Once in the workforce of the Merengues, a change of scenery for him, the young kid suddenly found himself thrust into the midst of a plethora of Galacticos. Nobody could have imagined then that during the next decade 'KB9' would plough his own furrow to become a legend in his own right. To last so long in such a club is testament to a foolproof adaptability and ability to bounce back at every moment.

Over several seasons the peak of his personal success was very much around Karim's agreement with Cristiano Ronaldo. While the Portuguese brought goals and glamour to Real, the child of Bron was Ronaldo's model teammate during those golden seasons when they won four Champions Leagues together.

Upon arrival at Bernabéu 'CR7' spent most of his time on the left flank, leaving the point of the attack to the Frenchman. Then, over time, the Portuguese folded his wings, settling at the top of the pyramid and leaving it to Benzema to ensure support and move away from the penalty area. An altruistic player, the ex-Lyonnais never took offence and was quick to stifle media speculation. 'Stop saying that I sacrifice myself for Cristiano; it's nonsense!' a passionate Benzema stated loudly and clearly. 'I like to play, I like football. It's not complicated to understand.'

Until March 2016 Didier Deschamps also defended his striker against all odds, even though many doubted Benzema's abilities would be translated into the major events on the world stage. Convinced of his hotshot, the coach announced that 'All the countries envy him,' but the issues involving the player in the Valbuena affair later cooled the ardour of the boss . . .

. . . That was, until Euro 2020, when Benzema was finally called up to join the ranks of the French team and made a welcome return following a substantial number of goals at club level. To cap it all, Benzema then claimed the 2022 Ballon d'Or as the best player in the world. He joined the European exodus to Saudi Arabia for the 2023–24 signing for Al-Ittihad.

TURKEY

Hakan
ÇALHANOĞLU

BORN: 8 February 1994, Mannheim, Germany

HEIGHT: 1.78 m

POSITION: Midfielder

PROFESSIONAL CAREER:
Karlsruher SC,
Hamburger SV,
Bayer 04 Leverkusen,
AC Milan,
Inter Milan

Transferring from one Milan club to another is a pretty daring feat, but that is the history of Hakan Çalhanoğlu. When the Turkish midfielder arrived at Inter Milan from rivals AC, the club was coming off the title of Italian champions and had just replaced outgoing coach Antonio Conte with Simone Inzaghi. It wasn't all plain sailing, though: far from welcoming Çalhanoğlu as a new messiah of the midfield, the Inter tifosi did not have much faith in the playmaker's abilities. Some thought his signing was a mistake by the club: 'When I asked the management to recruit him it was a risk,' Inzaghi admitted. 'The fans didn't really understand this choice, but I was convinced that he was the perfect player for us.'

After a sensational first two seasons the man christened 'Magic Hakan' had become arguably the best player in his position in the league. As a figure on the field he appears quiet, almost remote, but as soon as his boot touches the ball everything changes. He has the ability to speed up the game without running and dictates without shouting. He sees what others do not, and he plays early and with purpose. 'What I like is controlling the game, not chasing,' Çalhanoğlu revealed.

Hakan's career began in Germany, at Karlsruher SC, then he shone at Hamburg before joining Bayer Leverkusen. He quickly stood out for his technique and above all for how he strikes the ball. At Leverkusen a velvet touch allowed his delivery to make the difference at set pieces. Serie A clubs came circling, and in 2017 he signed for Italian giants AC Milan. At Milanello he discovered a club in a tough situation but not giving in to panic.

He backed himself on the pitch and reinvented himself as a more strategic leader, before in 2021 signing with rivals Inter Milan. Under Inzaghi he flourished, becoming a metronomic midfield general. As a holding midfielder in front of the defence, the regista allowed Çalhanoğlu countless touches, directing the play and prompting attacks from deep. He also weighed in with goals.

In 2023 Çalhanoğlu was an elegant part of the Inter team that made it to the Champions League final against Manchester City, where Çalhanoğlu confirmed his new status as the team's technical and mental leader. It's a trait he takes into his international role, where with Turkey he embodies experience, discipline and creativity.

DID YOU KNOW?

In 2013, while playing as a young player at Karlsruher SC in the German third division, Hakan Çalhanoğlu scored a goal directly from a free kick from his own half. The ball lobbed the opposing goalkeeper and flew into the net, astounding everyone. 'I saw the goalkeeper move forward and I tried without thinking,' he said. This crazy goal attracted the attention of the big clubs and launched his reputation as a master of set pieces. Since then, scoring from distance has become Hakan's signature move.

FRANCE

Eduardo

CAMAVINGA

BORN: 10 November 2002
Cabinda, Angola

HEIGHT: 1.82 m

POSITION: Midfielder

PROFESSIONAL CAREER:
Stade Rennais FC,
Real Madrid

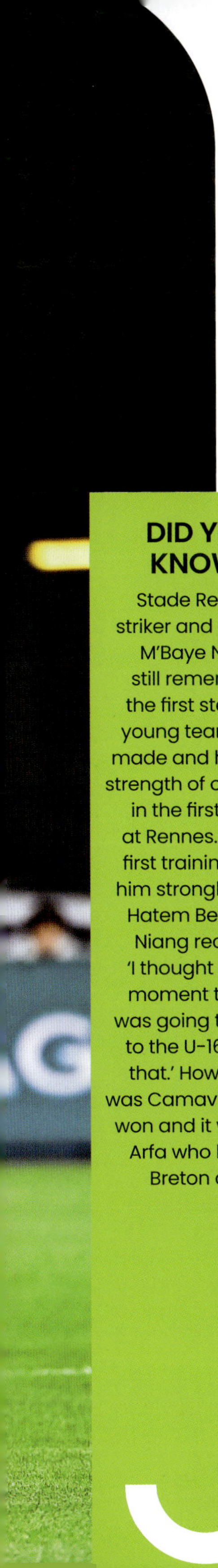

Having barely played in Ligue 1, it was evident early on that Eduardo Camavinga would not be lingering long in the French top flight, and that was confirmed in August 2021 when Real Madrid came knocking to swoop for the talented midfielder. Since his first appearance with the Stade Rennais in April 2019, Camavinga has been amazing the football world. At a time when records are being swallowed up by the precociously talented Kylian Mbappé, we will probably have to make some space for someone who obtained their French naturalisation shortly before Christmas 2019. A native of Cabinda in Angola, Camavinga quickly became an object of desire for Les Blues.

Eduardo seems to have no limits; his maturity and calmness are amazing at such a young age. Bred in Brittany, this terrier found coach Julien Stéphan, who launched Camavinga's career at the age of 15, and his assistant Mathieu Le Scornet, who had spotted him at the Ploumagoar tournament five years earlier. The trio was reunited and confident this would be a win-win for all involved.

At 17 years and 35 days Camavinga became the youngest player to score with Rennes in the top flight since the post-war period when he struck against Olympique Lyonnais, breaking on the counterattack to score what proved to be the match-winning goal. His outstanding achievements at both ends of the pitch demonstrated the full extent of the possibilities of this young combatant.

He defends with ice in his veins in a crowded penalty area and then shows composure at the other end to deceive the opposition goalkeeper, bluffing and annoying throughout. Goodbye and thank you, signed Camavinga. But perhaps his greatest strength is surely to succeed in still surprising people who have known him for a long time.

During Camavinga's years at AGL Drapeau-Fougères and his training at Stade Rennes all his educators praised his talent and ability to adapt to the next level. The question is no longer whether he is already part of a group of precocious talents such as Yoann Gourcuff or Ousmane Dembélé, who left their mark on the history of Rennes. The answer is a resounding 'Yes'. It's Real Madrid who is the winner, the signing of Camavinga surely the prelude to more silverware to fill the trophy cabinet.

DID YOU KNOW?

Stade Rennais striker and captain M'Baye Niang still remembers the first steps his young teammate made and his great strength of character in the first team at Rennes. 'For his first training I saw him strongly tackle Hatem Ben Arfa,' Niang recalled. 'I thought at that moment that he was going to return to the U-16s after that.' However, it was Camavinga who won and it was Ben Arfa who left the Breton club.

FRANCE

Rayan
CHERKI

BORN: 17 August 2003, Lyon, France

HEIGHT: 1.77 m

POSITION: Attacking midfielder, winger

PROFESSIONAL CAREER: Lyon B, Lyon, Manchester City FC

Karim Benzema, Hatem Ben Arfa, Nabil Fekir and Houssem Aouar: Lyon's breeding ground has been fertile in creating genius footballers. Is Olympique Lyonnais' nursery an inexhaustible factory of champions? Well, if the latest future jewel is a sign of the continuing churn of talent then the answer might be 'Yes.' Rayan Cherki was touted as a precocious talent from an early age. Outclassing all his teammates in all age categories, the OL star has never been short of ideas with a ball at his feet.

At the age of 16 years and 140 days he became the youngest player to score for the Rhone club in an official competition, netting during a Coupe de France match. It was a goal very much in his own image, a subtle left-footed drive that demonstrated the delicious technique of the Lyonnais technician. It came as no surprise to those who had watched his progression.

At six years old little Rayan managed the ball to perfection, and after accompanying his father to Lyon his talent opened the door to the Lyon Youth Academy, where he thrived. It was soon obvious that Cherki was superior to his peers: not only were his skills obvious in his age group, but he also stood out when promoted to the higher categories. He showed superb technical ability in one-on-one situations and unforgettable flashes of his talent as he plundered plenty of goals.

Big European clubs such as Manchester United began to take an interest but his idol, Juninho, freshly inducted as sporting director at Lyon, locked Cherki into his first professional contract. Manager Rudi Garcia, also recently arrived, then launched him into the big time.

There was no question of burning out the little prodigy, because even though Lyon was struggling with a cascade of injuries it was impossible to hold back his prodigious skill set. He was thrust into action, making his professional debut in a 0–0 Ligue 1 draw against Dijon on 19 October 2019. A move appeared inevitable after a string of virtuoso performances, and after impressing in Lyon's run to the quarter finals of the Europa League in 2025 he was snapped up by Manchester City.

Now serving under the tutelage of Pep Guardiola, Cherki is expected to shine, growing his burgeoning reputation and becoming a key player for both club and country, the latter for whom he made his debut against Spain in the 2025 Nations League.

DID YOU KNOW?

It was in a car park that Cherki caught the eye of football manager Gérard Houllier. Arriving with his big brother, little Rayan got out of the car with his ball and started a series of running juggles. In doing so he crossed paths with Jean-Michel Aulas, Lyon's sporting adviser, who asked to speak with his father. 'You have a 95 per cent chance of playing for OL one day,' Houllier predicted. The following Wednesday Rayan participated in a talent scouting day, and so began his rapid ascent.

ITALY

Federico
CHIESA

BORN: 25 October 1997
Genoa, Italy

HEIGHT: 1.75 m

POSITION: Winger

PROFESSIONAL CAREER:
ACF Fiorentina, Juventus FC,
Liverpool FC

DID YOU KNOW?

Twenty-two years apart, the legendary Italian goalkeeper Gianluigi Buffon won the Italian Cup with both the father and then with the son! In 1999, in the Parma jersey, 'Gigi' won the trophy alongside Enrico Chiesa against Fiorentina over two legs (1–1 and 2–2). With Juventus in 2021 the 2006 world champion conquered the Holy Grail again, climbing to the top step of the podium and taking up a position near Federico Chiesa after overcoming Atalanta 2–1.

The perfect archetype of the modern striker, the young transalpine Federico Chiesa is the king of timing his penalty box entries. Able to carry around the whole front of the attack, he also positionally looks like a nine and a half. 'Technically, on the left flank, I can transplant towards the axis, while on the right I try to go along the sideline before delivering a decisive pass,' this child of the ball insisted.

A good dribbler, excellent on set pieces and with superb peripheral vision despite long being criticised for playing with his head down, 'Pepo' knows how to rectify any situation. In his blood the native of Genoa has champion genes, his father Enrico having been an international with the Nerazzurri from 1996 to 2001. Born in Liguria, little Federico nevertheless made his first steps in Tuscany, near Florence, where his dad slammed in goal after goal in the Viola jersey of Fiorentina.

It is moreover at Fiorentina that the youngster did the majority of his classes. A good student, 'Fede' Chiesa had an excellent attitude to his studies. At the same time as football, he attended the University of Florence. Before skipping ahead, though, it is fair to remember that Chiesa Junior started with the primavera of Fiorentina in August 2016 before being launched into the seething duels of Serie A by Paulo Sousa.

Despite some up and down performances Chiesa got along perfectly with Croatian striker Nikola Kalinić and Federico Bernardeschi. A few months later the valuable advice of Franck Ribéry in training also helped him progress.

After making his way through the Italian youth ranks, Roberto Mancini gave Chiesa his first cap in March 2018 against Argentina, a 0–2 defeat. Well aware of the talent of the new generation, the head coach turned Chiesa into one of his jokers in the pack, and he was named as part of the Team of the Tournament at the delayed Euro 2020, in which Italy emerged triumphant.

In October 2020 Chiesa's departure for Juventus raised as many hopes as doubts. The Turin giants invested more than €50 million in Chiesa and in the peninsula some find the investment excessive; however, the perfectionist quickly silenced all his sceptics. Chiesa proved to be an exceptional signing for the Old Lady, settling into the squad and performing at elite levels on a weekly basis. However, he later fell out of favour and made the switch to the English Premier League and Liverpool, making his Reds debut in the Champions League win over AC Milan back in Italy.

FRANCE

Kingsley COMAN

BORN: 13 June 1996
Paris, France

HEIGHT: 1.81 m

POSITION: Winger

PROFESSIONAL CAREER:
Paris Saint-Germain FC,
Juventus FC,
Bayern Munich, Al-Nassr FC

Don't make him say what he doesn't think, but the departure of the two veterans Arjen Robben and Franck Ribéry at Bayern Munich finally freed up some space. Admittedly, competition has never scared Kingsley Coman, but the Parisian often had to start from scratch to sneak into a well-established workforce.

The fault of myriad injuries that hampered his young career, while the boy had the ability and instinct to shine his evolution looks like a roller coaster. Despite his reserved nature his teammates in the changing room appreciate the Frenchman. Consider this quote from David Alaba: 'King has the potential to quickly become a world-class player. I have rarely seen a guy so fast with ball at the foot.' Coman's style, which is all-in power and velocity punctuated by dazzling feints, is a feast for the eyes.

After arriving in Bavaria in 2015, having discovered football abroad from the age of 18 with Juventus, Kingsley Coman crossed paths with five renowned coaches. If the first time with Carlo Ancelotti was not the easiest, the native of Guadeloupe found a certain calmness on the left flank after passing under the watch of Pep Guardiola on the Bavarian bench before flourishing under the charismatic Jupp Heynckes. The experienced and influential German technician placed him on the right track. 'In particular, I told Kingsley to raise the head before centring and, sometimes, be better at managing his efforts.'

Initially loaned to Bayern, the French international was relieved when the Roten executives exercised the purchase option two seasons later. This meant he could quietly settle in the family home in Starnberg, by the lake. It's clear that Coman loves the club and the area, and winning seven titles with the Bavarian giants indicates he hasn't rested on his laurels. He has mastered the game more along with the language of Goethe.

Faced with repeated physical problems in recent seasons, consistency is the key for Coman. A move was on the horizon for the silky winger and in August 2025 he swapped Bavaria for Saudi Arabia, agreeing to a three-year contract with Saudi Pro-League side Al-Nassr, where he is sure to become a firm favourite with his new supporters!

DID YOU KNOW?

A product of the PSG training centre, Kingsley Coman almost never joined the Camp des Loges. He mentioned that, at the time a nine-year-old kid, he lived with his parents more than 60 kilometres away in Moissy-Cramayel in the south of Seine-et-Marne. That was simply too far! Educated at the Parisian school Yves Gergaud, despite the scepticism of its leaders Coman ended up convincing them that the gifted can achieve wonders. And, even if he couldn't attend all training sessions, the 'King' was firmly established every weekend in the team and lit up every game.

BELGIUM

Thibaut

COURTOIS

BORN: 11 May 1992
Bree, Belgium

HEIGHT: 2.00 m

POSITION: Goalkeeper

PROFESSIONAL CAREER:
KRC Genk,
Club Atlético de Madrid,
Chelsea FC, Real Madrid

DID YOU KNOW?

Rififi in the land of Tintin! After leaving his post as Belgian coach Marc Wilmots attacked the Courtois family, accusing the father, Thierry, of having revealed to the press some of his starting 11. 'I just have a problem when I finalise my selection at 6 pm and that at 6.15 pm it is made public. It means that a player has "sold" the selection. I learned that it was Thibaut's dad who did it.' Courtois' father and son have decided to file a complaint for defamation.

Thibaut Courtois finished as the best goalkeeper in the 2018 World Cup according to the Fédération Internationale de Football Association (FIFA), claiming the Golden Glove award, but that was of little consolation to the giant Belgian as his team was sent packing at the semi-final stage, a victim of France's march to the title. Les Bleus won the last-four match 1–0. Courtois found it all hard to digest, his bitterness at the defeat doing the rounds on social networks.

As soon as the failure at Saint-Petersburg was confirmed the Limburger let loose, first in the media of his country: 'It was a frustrating game. France did not play. She only defended with eleven players behind,' was his curt assessment. Even more infuriating was that it was a defender, in this case Samuel Umtiti, who put an end to the Belgian dream from a set piece. The Flemish giant did not expect the slingshot that ensued.

We could almost forget that the doorman of Brée reacted hotly in the grip of disappointment. The day before the final, as France got set to play Croatia, Thibaut Courtois diplomatically corrected the situation. 'I'm sorry if I expressed myself a little loudly,' he said. 'At Les Bleus, I know Griezmann, Kanté. I wish them victory.'

Turning around, the number 1 from Quiévrain also realised that his Belgium team had played the same tactics in defeating Brazil in a memorable match. He was exceptional during the quarter final against the Seleção, achieving no less than nine saves that included the last breathtaking one in extra time, tipping away a curling shot from Neymar. Despite the Red Devils' rearguard action, no Brazilian deplored the Belgians' approach to the fixture.

On his line Thibaut Courtois has many admirers, his stature and ball retention sure under pressure and his anticipation and ability to get down low when necessary belying his 2-metre frame. Under the stewardship of the defensively resolute Diego Simeone at Atlético de Madrid and Antonio Conte at Chelsea, Courtois was a rock behind teams that set up in a defensive block. Today, even at a more open and fluid Real Madrid, the rampart of Limburg has lost nothing of his imposing presence.

BELGIUM

Kevin
DE BRUYNE

BORN: 28 June 1991
Tronchiennes, Belgium

HEIGHT: 1.81 m

POSITION: Midfielder

PROFESSIONAL CAREER:
KRC Genk,
SV Werder Bremen,
Chelsea FC,
VfL Wolfsburg,
Manchester City FC,
SSC Napoli

It is a headache for a coach, albeit a welcome one, that this capable Belgian is able to play in all positions in front of a defence and beyond, but no manager has had cause to complain – apart from maybe José Mourinho – about the benefit of such a midfield wonder. Long underrated, Kevin De Bruyne is now seen as a formidable game winner. He has learned when to run and when to release, and has evolved into a world-class operator.

'I love it when he evolves into a fake number 10,' Eric Gerets, the former Belgian coach of Olympique de Marseille, said. 'He is both able to score and distribute decisive passes.' However, it wasn't all rosy in the garden of the Red Devils either. During Euro 2016 De Bruyne and the Walloon, Eden Hazard, tiptoed through the matches, with Belgium increasingly being put under the magnifying glass. A shame when you have such talents.

'We love to play together, even if some people think it's not possible,' Hazard, who was visibly offended at the accusation that the duo could not combine in the national team, said. 'I am convinced that we are compatible. I'm more of a percussion player; Kevin is able to create breaches, to hit from afar.'

The result was more convincing during the World Cup in Russia in 2018, with Belgium installed on the third step of the podium albeit with the usual complaints from the media. 'Are you going to talk to me about my position in selection until the end of my career?' an annoyed De Bruyne asked. 'I play where the coach asks me, for the good of the team. It is not a question of freedom, but of space!'

Since reaching his peak at Manchester City, the data is better defined with Pep Guardiola. Thanks to his ability to occupy all the positions of midfield and attack in the same match, 'KDB' is a bit like an extension of the magician Guardiola's brain. 'Kevin is one of the best players I have ever seen, because he knows how to do everything, absolutely everything,' Guardiola insisted. 'He is a stable guy who loves the game and lives for it. He is so smart! He understands everything right away. He goes fast and sees space better than anyone.'

His City love affair couldn't last forever, and in the summer of 2025 it was revealed that De Bruyne would be moving to pastures new. A clutch of clubs vied for his signature, but it was Italian Champions Napoli that won the day.

DID YOU KNOW?

Not many players have stood up to José Mourinho. When he returned to Chelsea in the summer of 2013 after his loan to Werder Bremen, Kevin De Bruyne did not allow himself to become fazed with the spiky attention of the Portuguese coach. 'He had said in the press that I was not making the effort in training,' De Bruyne commented. 'It's easy to say that when nobody's around to check since the meetings are on camera, but everyone knows I'm not like that.' Have some of that!

THE NETHERLANDS

Frenkie
DE JONG

BORN: 12 May 1997
Arkel,
The Netherlands

HEIGHT: 1.80 m

POSITION: Midfielder

PROFESSIONAL CAREER:
Willem II Tilburg,
Jong Ajax,
Ajax Amsterdam,
FC Barcelona

At ASV Arkel in the outer suburbs east of Rotterdam, where it all started for him, Frenkie de Jong was surprised to learn that his former coaches had, for a time, considered using his first name on a tribune of their small stadium. The interested party refused on the pretext that he had not yet accomplished anything as a footballer.

Maybe not yet, but the strategist is no longer a stranger to the football world and especially since his international debut – which coincided with the return to the forefront of the game for the Netherlands, who had been plunged in mothballs for a few months – and also since his exploits with Ajax and, above all, his sensational transfer to FC Barcelona.

After a head-to-head showdown with PSG over the acquisition of de Jong, Barça won the bidding with a contract for five seasons. The amount of the operation was €75 million, plus €11 million in bonuses. The French world champions discovered de Jong's class one evening in autumn 2018 when they stalled in front of so much genius. 'I was going to hurry him, but I never managed to get near him,' Antoine Griezmann summarised.

Excellent with the ball, the pillar of the renewed Oranje is one of those players who spends the most time looking to play forward. Whether it be the long game or the short game, everything seems easy for the prodigy. Often compared with Frank Rijkaard, he is also deified as a modern-time Franz Beckenbauer. In the local press he became the 'Kaiser d'Arkel'.

As a junior player it was already impossible to steal the ball from de Jong. At the time the size of a barely blooming tulip, he was sold to the academy of Ajax for . . . €1! His father, who was crazy about new-wave music and an absolute fan of the band Frankie Goes to Hollywood, named Frenkie after the group. In his bedroom little de Jong cut out posters and collected all Barça-related items. His role model was Sergio Busquets: he only had eyes for the great Catalan machine and spent time dissecting the slightest of his gestures.

Despite the fortune awaiting him at Barça and overwhelming popularity, 'FDJ', who partied in Amsterdam at the completion of an unforgettable cup championship double at the conclusion of his time in the Netherlands, promised to return to Arkel from time to time. It's good to remember your history, recharge your batteries and keep your feet on the ground.

DID YOU KNOW?

Before he had even donned the Barça jersey, Frenkie de Jong had made the sworn enemy – Real Madrid – cry. After an amazing victory by Ajax in March 2019 at Santiago Bernabéu, the Dutchman went to find his relatives in a hotel in Madrid. As related by the great Dutch daily *De Telegraaf*, he was welcomed by his family on his arrival and his parents quipped: 'Now you can really go to Barcelona!' No doubt the Camp Nou aficionados enjoyed that one!

THE NETHERLANDS

Matthijs

DE LIGT

BORN: 12 August 1999
Leiderdorp,
The Netherlands

HEIGHT: 1.89 m

POSITION: Defender

PROFESSIONAL CAREER:
Jong Ajax, Ajax Amsterdam, Juventus FC, Bayern Munich, Manchester United FC

When you're aged 15 and you've already been named best player of tournaments reserved for the U-17s and then for the U-19s, there is obviously something special. It must be said, therefore, that the young Matthijs de Ligt enjoyed a rapid rise, imposing himself without any fear in the Ajax youth squad.

In September 2016 he started with the big boys, with a first match in the Eredivisie, the Dutch championship, against Willem II Tilburg, and he even scored a goal to celebrate his debut with Ajax, who triumphed 5–0. The new pearl from South Holland became, after Clarence Seedorf, the youngest scorer in the iconic Amsterdam jersey. It was a supersonic ascent for this incredible talent.

As a child and with racquet in hand he dreamed of following in the footsteps of Roger Federer or Rafael Nadal on the tennis courts, but it was football that claimed him. For this lifelong Ajax fan the first chills at the Johan Cruijff ArenA occurred when he was small. His father took him to follow his idols and he watched with stars in his eyes. He even posed for a photo with Luis Suárez, the ace goal grabber, on a match night when he was a ball boy.

At the school of the Lancers he surprised the coaches with his sense of investment in everything he did and his courage. Matthijs de Ligt never backed down, even when faced with opponents craftier than him. Did he develop this confidence when he, the big brother, defended his little brother Wouter and his twin sisters in the schoolyard?

In any case, the kid from FC Abcoude was still ahead of others. Full of confidence, the new captain imposed himself as a true leader in the midst of babies who would go on to charm Europe during the 2018–19 season. After overturning both Real Madrid and Juventus, Ajax just failed at the gates of the final against Tottenham Hotspur in the last four but won the double at home. Suddenly, the Lancers entered the hearts of the supporters.

It was no coincidence either that after their painful absences from Euro 2016 and the 2018 World Cup the Oranje armada was back in force, with Matthijs de Ligt as one of the most powerful and important representatives. A transfer to European giants Bayern Munich confirmed his burgeoning reputation, before a move to English behemoth Manchester United for the start of the 2024–25 season gave De Ligt another chance to stake a claim as one of the continent's best defenders.

DID YOU KNOW?

The 'little fat one' almost never set foot on the grounds of the Ajax training centre. At eight years of age the child was obviously a gifted football player – that's a fact – but the kid was also somewhat chubby. He was even nicknamed 'Bolle', Dutch for meatball or dumpling. Finally, after almost 12 months of hesitation, the green light was given for de Ligt to join the legendary Amsterdam club. 'When I landed there,' the blond colossus remembered, 'I was taken directly to a dietitian and placed on a diet!'

FRANCE

Ousmane
DEMBÉLÉ

BORN: 15 May 1997
Vernon, France

HEIGHT: 1.78 m

POSITION: Winger

PROFESSIONAL CAREER:
Stade Rennais FC,
Borussia Dortmund,
FC Barcelona,
Paris Saint-Germain FC

DID YOU KNOW?

The current coach of Stade Rennais, Julien Stéphan, has long blooded Ousmane Dembélé in the Breton formation. The Rouge et Noir coach mastered his 'Dembouz' into a line-up that fulfilled his potential. 'It is more to his advantage if we play in a 4-3-3, because he is covered, he has less effort to make in recovery and thus repositions higher up the pitch. This allows him to express all his qualities in offensive transitions when space becomes available. There, he enjoys it!'

'I quit football!' It was through this shocking SMS in June 2015 that Ousmane Dembélé warned René Ruello, then president of Stade Rennes, of his dissatisfaction. Exasperated by the fact that his coach Philippe Montanier did not believe in him the young attacker, despite his youthful 18 years, showed a strong backbone.

Everything ended up going back to normal but, convinced of his own ability at the game, the gifted Norman, whose father is of Malian origin, and his mum, of Senegalese-Mauritanian origin, had to quickly learn the ropes. Capable of punching through any defence with his pace and footwork, Dembouz acquired this technique as a teenager when he flourished playing futsal.

At the age of 13 he was headed for Stade Rennais. His burst of speed, combined with his ease of bringing danger into opposition territory whenever he got possession of the ball, worked wonders. Good with both feet, the freakish ability to take on and more often than not beat his marker, leant some to accuse him of unnecessary dribbling and holding on to the ball too long. Shrugging off his critics, Dembélé approached life in Ligue 1 like an old veteran, accelerating his career to such an extent that he played barely 30 matches in the French top flight.

A transfer to Germany in the summer of 2016 followed, to the powerhouse of Borussia Dortmund, then coached by Thomas Tuchel, before an international debut for Les Bleus against the Cote d'Ivoire in a 0-0 draw in Lens. A fan of French cartoon *Olive and Tom*, Dembélé shows some of the characteristics of the duo, often employing sensational tricks and skills while playing the game with a smile on his face. His time in the Bundesliga showed his fierce work ethic as well, but the atmosphere became tense in the off-season.

Seduced by the prospect of a move to Spain and FC Barcelona, Ousmane came into conflict with the coaches of the Schwarzgelben who, understandably, were loath to lose one of their star prospects. Finally, Dembélé won his case and headed for Camp Nou.

Dembélé's Barca career was a frustrating one: despite brief glimpses of form and his undoubted class and ability, he was never able to settle at the Blaugrana. A switch to the bright lights of Paris, and PSG, will not lessen the limelight but might provide the home comforts he craves.

PORTUGAL

Rúben
DIAS

BORN: 14 May 1997
Amadora, Portugal

HEIGHT: 1.86 m

POSITION: Defender

PROFESSIONAL CAREER:
SL Benfica,
Manchester City FC

DID YOU KNOW?

There was a funny welcome for Rúben Dias in October 2020 at Elland Road, the home stadium of Leeds United. Getting off the bus, the young Citizens defender was turned away by the security service because they had not recognised the Portuguese international. Before this Premier League match Dias had to wait for a member of staff to verify his identity before he could enter the changing room. Manchester City FC left Marcelo Bielsa's Leeds with a point in a 1–1 draw.

Rúben Dias certainly knows how to make an impression at the highest level: a sensational performance against Paris Saint-Germain during the Champions League semi-final in 2021 is testament to that. In the first leg of that last-four encounter at the Parc des Princes and in tandem with John Stones, Dias was able to stifle the talents of Kylian Mbappé and company, a performance by the Portuguese defender that warmed the hearts of Citizens supporters.

Even if the epic run to the final ended in a feeling of unfinished business, City beaten in Dias's home country of Portugal when they lost the all-English showdown to Chelsea 0–1 in Porto, the stature and reputation of the committed centre back certainly grew. In a wink to fate, Dias grew up in Amadora only a stone's throw away from the Luz stadium, the mythical stadium of Benfica.

A nascent star in his youth from local side Estrela, Rúben joined the Eagles academy at the age of 11. With an old head on young shoulders he showed dazzling maturity for his age, and his coaches particularly appreciated his ability to stay focused for 90 minutes without relaxation. With a physique that belied his tender years, it was little surprise that he turned professional with the Lisbon giants as soon as he was eligible to sign.

Dias made his debut for Benfica in September 2017 against Rui Vitória in the domestic championship and his ascent was rapid. Later that year he rubbed shoulders with Marcus Rashford and Romelu Lukaku during a gala match against Manchester United. Despite the defeat against the Red Devils, 0–1, his immaculate performance did not go unnoticed. Unsurprisingly, the native of Amadora was swiftly on the radar of Portuguese coach Fernando Santos, Dias making the Portugal squad for the 2018 World Cup after excelling in the youth grades.

The former captain of the Portugal youth side didn't see a minute of playing time in Russia, but that did not dim his light. A year later, placed alongside José Fonte in the heart of the defence, Dias was a major part of the Nations Cup triumph against the Netherlands, Portugal winning 1–0. That was quickly followed in September 2020 by a thunderous announcement: Dias was off to the Premier League, Manchester City taking out the chequebook and investing €68 million to bring Dias to the north of England. At the end of his first season in England he was voted the best player by the local Manchester press. The only other Portuguese to win this award was Cristiano Ronaldo, twice: 2007 and 2008.

COLUMBIA

Luis
DÍAZ

BORN: 13 January 1997
Barrancas, Columbia

HEIGHT: 1.80 m

POSITION: Winger

PROFESSIONAL CAREER:
Barranquilla FC,
Atlético Junior, FC Porto,
Liverpool FC,
Bayern Munich

A true revelation of the Champions League semi-final in Villarreal in May 2022, the Colombian winger playing for Liverpool was simply unstoppable: that evening in Spain he conquered everyone. Displaying his full range of dizzying tricks and skills on the left flank of the Reds attack, Díaz ran rings around the defenders of the 'Yellow Submarine'. After arriving at Liverpool just months earlier, Luis Fernando Díaz Marulanda burst into the hearts of fans of the English club.

With his incessant running, terrific close control and dribbling skills and his enigmatic approach to taking on defenders, the former Barranquilla winger quickly became an adopted Scouser and had head coach Jürgen Klopp raving about his abilities. Díaz had landed in Liverpool in January 2022, signed from FC Porto, where he had spent just two and a half years following his rapid transition to European football, and penned a long-term contract with one of the giants of the game.

It was a great reward for Díaz, who is a big fan of Ronaldinho, and he was spotted in his country by a certain Carlos Valderrama. The former Colombian international and Montpellier legend spotted the budding Díaz in his homeland during a tournament that brought together amateurs, with the players all being from local ethnicities. The goal was to ascertain the best selection to compete in an indigenous version of the Copa América.

Luis Díaz comes from a Wayuu family, a Native American ethnic group that lives on the border with Venezuela. Some have rejected social contact. The future champion grew up in poverty, and to escape he needed to become a wizard with the ball at his feet. Little Díaz dared, tried and succeeded, with Valderrama taking him to Barranquilla FC. Nicknamed 'El Fideo' (the noodle) because of his slender appearance, the winger lit up the national stage with a range of superb matches.

In September 2018 Díaz marked his first international selection for Colombia against Argentina in a 0–0 draw, and once in the team he didn't leave the group again. At the age of 21 he played in the final of the Copa Sudamericana with Atlético Junior, although they lost against the Brazilians from Club Athletico Paranaense. However, it wasn't a defeat that hindered his departure to Europe: he played for Porto before signing with Liverpool in 2022. He helped them win the FA Cup, League Cup (twice) and Premier League title before signing with Bayern Munich in 2025 for a fee reported to be worth €75 million.

DID YOU KNOW?

During the Copa América 2021 held in Brazil, Luis Díaz, with four goals, won the title of top scorer in the South American tournament alongside a renowned player – and not just any, since it was Lionel Messi! If the Argentine star ended up winning this 47th edition of the tournament, then the little Colombian was more than satisfied with the third step on the podium. During the classification match against Peru, which Los Cafeteros won 3–2, Díaz helped himself to a double.

ITALY

Gianluigi DONNARUMMA

BORN: 25 February 1999
Castellammare di Stabia,
Italy

HEIGHT: 1.96 m

POSITION: Goalkeeper

PROFESSIONAL CAREER:
AC Milan,
Paris Saint-Germain FC,
Manchester City FC

DID YOU KNOW?

His jersey number of a double 9 is not very common in the pantheon of goalkeepers, who are usually accustomed to a small number, but Donnarumma wears the number 99 simply in reference to his year of birth. He was born 25 February 1999 and became the second youngest goalkeeper to play in Serie A, ahead of monumental talents such as Gianluigi Buffon.

A teenager among the professionals! The first steps that Gianluigi Donnarumma made in taking his place between the posts for AC Milan perfectly illustrate an old coach's catchphrase: in the world of football, if you're good enough you're old enough. For the native of Castellammare di Stabia, a town located in the Gulf of Naples, life as a footballer was always at full speed ahead.

When Donnarumma joined the Napoli academy at the age of four, the kid who had gold between his hands was already dreaming of appearing in the famous red and black like his 'uncle' Ernesto, a fervent supporter of the Milanese club. It wasn't all plain sailing for the young stopper, as his incredible performances along with his huge frame – sometimes he was as much as 30 cm taller than his peers – led to suspicious looks from opponents each week. This obliged his mother Marinella to present his birth certificate every weekend to dispel any doubts as to his eligibility.

Very quickly the talent of the young goalkeeper crossed the borders of the Campania, spreading far and wide, with Juventus, Fiorentina, Roma and Udinese sending their scouts to try to secure the signature of the prodigy. However, 'Gigio' had already chosen his destination: AC Milan, where his brother Antonio, nine years his senior, was already evolving into a classy goalkeeper.

At Milanello the rise of the young hopeful, voted best goalkeeper of the European Under-18 Championship at just 17 years of age, was dazzling. Imperious in the air, endowed with excellent reflexes and solid on his line, it did not take long for Donnarumma to impose himself in the first-team goal, relegating the incumbent, Spaniard Diego López, to the substitutes bench when Donnarumma was just 16 years and 9 months old.

A cap for the national team followed. Giampiero Ventura, the Italian coach, called him up for a friendly match against France. Brought on in the second half, Donnarumma replaced his idol, the legend Gianluigi Buffon, and once again broke a record as a precocious youth. Regularly cited among the best goalkeepers of both Italy and Europe, the Italian had plenty of envious eyes cast his way. Milan did their best to extend his contract, but when it ran down in 2021 Gianluigi Donnarumma joined Paris Saint-Germain and brought strong competition to Keylor Navas. After winning Euro 2020 with Italy the goalkeeper claimed the Champions League with PSG, then signed for Manchester City at the start of the 2025–26 season.

FRANCE

Désiré
DOUÉ

BORN: 3 June 2005, Angers, France

HEIGHT: 1.81 m

POSITION: Attacking midfielder, winger

PROFESSIONAL CAREER: Stade Rennais FC II, Stade Rennais FC, Paris Saint-Germain FC

In Rennes there was Camavinga, Doku, Tel and then him: Désiré Doué. Less exposed to the media glare than the others but just as electrifying, Désiré is not just the next cab off the rank. The skilful winger plays his football with a child-like enthusiasm but also with the care and diligence of a player in his 30s, where there is no such thing as a sense of panic.

Born in Angers into a family where football is almost a religion, it was his older brother Guéla who led the way. Joining the youth ranks of Rennes as a five year old, the raw ability of the youngster was noticeable from an early age and at 17 he was deemed ready for a professional debut, one that arrived without much fanfare. Suddenly, within a short period he made a series of appearances in Ligue 1, becoming entrenched in the 11 as though it had always been that way. Without a set position at that stage of his career Doué was used in a variety of roles. Each time he adapted and understood the positional requirements, learning everything rapidly and on the job.

Recruiters noted his name and scouts from across the English Channel were salivating with each piece of information they gathered about the prospect. Désiré, on the other hand, remained stoic. He talked about progress, patience and performance, not the transfer window. 'I'm at Rennes, I'm improving. Every game teaches me something. The rest we will see,' was his measured comment on all the talk surrounding him. In the stands Roazhon Park was stirred to its feet when Doué was in possession, and his accelerated rate of learning sounded a clarion call. The enticing sirens of PSG were eventually too much to ignore.

With Kylian Mbappé having left the French capital for Madrid, Doué arrived to replace him. Many thought it was a joke that this young gun had been hired to replace the irreplaceable, but a few months later no one was laughing anymore. In one year the Doué rocket exploded across the planet. Transferred for more than €50 million, he achieved a historic treble with his new club. A double goal scorer and involved in three goals in the Champions League final against Inter Milan, he became a world star.

At just 19 years of age, the youngest player in the 22 starters in that final went down in the history of the competition. An absolute fan of Neymar, he asked Brazilian player Marcelo, who came down to the Allianz Arena to present him with the player of the match award that evening, if he could convince Ney to follow him on Instagram. That same evening Doué had a new follower.

DID YOU KNOW?

Désiré Doué takes his name from his uncle, Noumandiez Désiré Doué, a former Ivorian legend of refereeing who officiated at the 2014 World Cup. He was the first Ivorian referee to participate in the competition and refereed two matches at the World Cup in Brazil, including one for Didier Deschamps' France team against Ecuador in Brasília. The match ended in a 0-0 draw. Since 2022 Noumandiez has been in charge of refereeing at the Confederation of African Football.

THE NETHERLANDS

Denzel

DUMFRIES

BORN: 18 April 1996, Rhoon, Netherlands

HEIGHT: 1.88 m

POSITION: Defender

PROFESSIONAL CAREER: Sparta Rotterdam, SC Heerenveen, PSV Eindhoven, Inter Milan

DID YOU KNOW?

In 2014, while still playing as an amateur in Barendrecht, Denzel Dumfries stated in an interview that he aspired to one day play for the national team of Aruba, his father's country of origin. He even honoured a friendly selection with them, but he quickly understood that he could aim higher and had to make a big decision: stay, or give up on Aruba to try his luck with the Netherlands. Three years later he was wearing the Oranje jersey.

Denzel Dumfries doesn't play on the edge: he plays in a permanent state of overflow. With each stride he makes the opponent retreat, and with each contact he imposes himself on the match. He might be a fullback, but he plays in an elegant yet bulldozing style. When he gets on the overlap it's with the purpose to hurt, and when he defends it's with the purpose to extinguish the opposition attacks. 'I'm not here to look pretty,' he said.

Dumfries was born in a working-class district of Rotterdam. The ball arrived early in his life; however, the path to success was anything but marked out. There was no prestigious academy for Dumfries, no dream all mapped out for him. He started as an amateur in Barendrecht, and although he was tall and strong he was still a little raw and it was said he might be too uncoordinated to go far. Dumfries said nothing, instead putting his head down and getting on with the work.

He played for Sparta Rotterdam, then emerged as a standout at Heerenveen and PSV Eindhoven. There he broke all the statistics for a fullback, developed into a leader and became a defensive monster. His selection with the Netherlands national team did not take long, and at Euro 2021 he caused a sensation: goals, decisive crosses and crazy runs. Dumfries was everywhere and the world noticed.

Inter Milan recruited him in 2021 to replace Achraf Hakimi and with that came enormous pressure, yet Dumfries took all of that in his stride and more, making the right side of the field his playground. His style was aggressive, unselfish and unfiltered. He could cross, score and defend, sometimes combining all three in the same action. Above all, he is inexhaustible.

In Milan he became key in the five-man defensive system, playing his part with unflinching relentlessness. He scored against Barça and shone against AC Milan, and the tifosi quickly adopted him as one of their own. 'When you play for Inter you feel history,' he said. 'You want to earn this jersey, every weekend.'

With the Netherlands Dumfries remains an indisputable part of the system. His connection with Frenkie de Jong and sharp runs make him a nightmare for the opposing wingers, and even if his style is sometimes criticised for a lack of finesse he could not care. 'The important thing is to be effective,' he stated.

ARGENTINA

Paulo

DYBALA

BORN: 15 November 1993
Laguna Larga, Argentina

HEIGHT: 1.77 m

POSITION: Forward

PROFESSIONAL CAREER:
Instituto de Córdoba, Palermo FC, Juventus FC, AS Roma

DID YOU KNOW?

In Argentina, Paulo Dybala is nicknamed 'El Pibe de la pensión' (the kid of the pension) because, on the death of his father, the gifted niño with a ball at his feet was taken in by the centre of training at the Instituto Atlético Central Córdoba. In order to prevent him from having a gruelling travel schedule on a daily basis – from his home to the training grounds – the club preferred to grant the adolescent a boarder status. In August 2011, at 17 years of age, he became a professional player there.

Of Polish origin by his paternal grandfather and Italian by his maternal grandmother, Paulo Bruno Exequiel Dybala was born in the city of Córdoba in the north of Argentina. It was at one of the best training clubs in the city, the Instituto, where he scored his first goals and earned himself the nickname of 'la Joya' (the Jewel) by those who first witnessed the blossoming of his talent.

While still just a teenager Dybala began to beat all known youth records at the club: youngest goal scorer, youngest player to appear in the first team, first 17-year-old player to register two hat-tricks and score in six matches in a row!

A little over a year later he left Argentina, departing for the land of his ancestors and joining the squad of US Palermo in Sicily. Once again the South American broke records at a dizzying speed, including becoming the youngest player to score in the Palermo shirt. In three seasons he scored 21 goals in 93 games and made others sit up and take notice of this emerging talent.

The jump was immediate, and in the summer of 2015 Dybala was off, headed to northern Italy to join the prestigious ranks of the 'Old Lady', Juventus. Always searching for those rare gems, Juventus bet on Dybala to raise the spirits of a club that was going through a beleaguered period of existence. At the Bianconeri, midfielder Paul Pogba christened a new nickname for the prodigy. His French partner called him 'Carré R2', alluding to the keys used in some famous video games for performing a curling strike.

It wasn't long before Dybala found himself lining up alongside another idol: Lionel Messi, in the colours of the Argentina national team, came off the bench for the Albiceleste to replace Carlos Tevez in a FIFA World Cup qualifying match against Paraguay.

During the 2018–19 season the Argentinian Jewel lost some of his lustre and began a drought in front of goal. Perhaps the arrival of Cristiano Ronaldo into the black and white stripes changed his role and cost him a starting spot. For some Dybala might not be the player he once was, but talent is boundless and a switch to AS Roma and a new lease of life under enigmatic coach José Mourinho might be the prelude to a return to his dazzling best.

SPAIN

Ansu

FATI

BORN: 31 October 2002
Bissau, Guinea-Bissau

HEIGHT: 1.78 m

POSITION: Forward

PROFESSIONAL CAREER:
FC Barcelona, Brighton & Hove Albion FC, AS Monaco (loan)

DID YOU KNOW?

Under Victor Valdés with the Juveniles Ansu Fati was more than pampered, but the former goalkeeper who became a coach remembered an incredible anecdote about the little wonder. 'During a tournament in Russia, he grimaced,' Valdes recalled. 'I told him to show me his boots, and their condition was disastrous. His pains came from there, so I bought him a new pair to make him feel better.'

'We are potentially facing a footballer who can mark the beginning of a new era. The new Messi? These are big words, but can he be a world-class footballer? The answer is "Yes".' These aren't the opinions of just anyone but the thoughts of the midfield maestro Xavi himself when asked about the sheer quality of the young superstar that is Ansu Fati. When the old brain of Barça pronounces things this way it is rarely said lightly.

In truth, FC Barcelona is betting a lot on its favourite son, torn from the clutches of its hereditary enemy Real Madrid, who offered fabulous terms to Ansu's father Bori Fati, himself a former footballer. 'Real offered more money than Barça but we chose Barcelona, because the Catalan recruiters came to us with the contract and convinced me,' he revealed. Why did the Blaugrana put so much faith in this phenomenon? Well, because he is just that!

Anssumane Fati – his real name – has extraordinary passion and a real sense of purpose, although that often appears confusing to many who watch him. His style of play and laidback demeanour belie his aggressive will to win. Born in Guinea-Bissau, Ansu lived in Spain from the age of six. He first strapped on his boots at CDF Herrera, the Andalusian team of the area where his parents lived. A few months later Sevilla FC noticed his rare ability and flexibility and promptly signed him up. It didn't stop there, though, and before he was even 10 years old he arrived at La Masia, the famed Barcelona academy.

Despite a double tibia/fibula fracture at the beginning of his adolescence, the gifted Fati skipped through the age ranks at a rapid pace. In July 2019 Ansu Fati extended his contract with the Catalan club until 2022, with a release clause already set at €100 million! In the weeks that followed, even before his 17th birthday he beat a long-term youth record both in Spain and in the Champions League by making his Barcelona debut.

After struggling to cement a place in the Barcelona line-up, Fati switched to English Premier League outfit Brighton where, under Roberto De Zerbi, he flourished in the top flight and impressed in the club's maiden European campaign in the UEFA Europa League. While the move didn't pan out as he would have hoped Fati has another chance at redemption, spending the 2025–26 campaign on loan in Ligue Un with AS Monaco.

PORTUGAL

João
FÉLIX

BORN: 10 November 1999
Viseu, Portugal

HEIGHT: 1.81 m

POSITION: Forward

PROFESSIONAL CAREER:
SL Benfica,
Atlético de Madrid,
Chelsea FC, FC Barcelona,
Chelsea FC, AC Milan,
Al-Nassr FC

DID YOU KNOW?

When he arrived at Atlético, João Félix wanted to wear the number 79 on his back; however, that request was denied because La Liga regulations require players to wear numbers between 1 and 25. Felix then attempted to claim the number 10 jersey but his wish was still not granted because Ángel Correa was assigned the lucky number. Finally, the young Portuguese received the number 7, which had been left vacant by Antoine Griezmann when he departed for Barcelona.

A pinch of Rui Costa for his technical side, a hint of Youri Djorkaeff for his position in the team as a nine and a half, a good dose of Kaká for his offensive impact and some grains of Michel Platini for his vision of the game: here is the excellent recipe that fell in July 2019 into the melting pot of Atlético de Madrid. It was for this combination of promise and ability that the Colchoneros broke their piggy bank.

It was some bet to enlist a 19-year-old kid, certainly supremely gifted but still far from the finished article. João Félix himself was not about to get carried away and was keen to keep a low profile. 'I have understood that there were high expectations around me, but I never saw it as a bad thing. I still have been very calm in this phase of adaptation. I had the support of my family and friends, in addition to that of Atlético. The €126 million fee is never in my mind.'

It must be said that the little marvel has amazed at every stage, starting from when he burst onto the stage as a young talent. From his first steps his parents Carla and Carlos used to hide trinkets and precious objects in the living room, which the young scoundrel would hunt down. He discovered life-sized football at FC Porto at the age of eight; however, the Dragons in one of their less-inspired moves did not rate him, insisting he was too small and weak. Therefore, as a teenager he was allowed to leave for the enemy Benfica, the club rubbing their hands in glee at their acquisition.

In September 2016 João Félix became the youngest player to start with the Eagles Reserves, at the age of 16 years and 312 days. In April 2019, despite his braces recalling the precocity of his youth, he netted a sublime hat-trick, all registered with ease and relaxation, against Eintracht Frankfurt in the Europa League.

A counterattack specialist armed with an elegant dribbling ability, Félix lived two huge moments that summer: he conquered the maiden Nations League with Seleção das Quinas, Portugal claiming the title, before his record-breaking transfer to Atlético. Félix accepted an offer from Chelsea on loan but failed to shine. FC Barcelona took a gamble on him, before a surprise return loan to Stamford Bridge in 2024–25. A shift to AC Milan in January 2025 failed to bring out his best; hopefully his time with Al-Nassr in Saudi Arabia is more fruitful.

PORTUGAL

Bruno FERNANDES

BORN: 8 September 1994
Maia, Portugal

HEIGHT: 1.79 m

POSITION: Midfielder

PROFESSIONAL CAREER:
Novara FC, Udinese Calcio, UC Sampdoria, Sporting CP, Manchester United FC

Be careful, as one Fernandes can hide another! On 10 November 2017 in Viseu in the 56th minute of a friendly between Portugal and Saudi Arabia, which the hosts won 1–0, Manuel Fernandes gave way to a newcomer Bruno Fernandes. It was a big step for the former student of Boavista, his trajectory seemingly ever on an upward curve.

To complete his training the 'Canon de Maia' (Maya's canon) – his nickname in his hometown – set sail at the age of 17 for Piedmont. He earned his junior stripes on the green grass of Novara Calcio, between Turin and Milan, not the normal hunting ground for a Portuguese youth. With his natural class and in a country marked by exceptional champions, the kid was quickly decked out with the nickname of 'little Maradona'.

Everything was moving at a rapid rate for Bruno but he was able to stand tall, showcasing his ability to always be well placed, have an eye for a pass and, despite his young age, have the lucidity without rushing to find the best path to goal for himself or for others. Despite this silk Fernandes still embraced steel, a style he was ready to assume for the good of the team.

'I am certainly a player who sacrifices themselves,' he said. 'Sometimes I know I exaggerate my actions on the field and give in to the pressure of the moment, but it's because I want to occupy every part of the field and be involved everywhere.' Fernandes discovered a high level of football in Serie B, but it was at Udinese that he first encountered the true elite of Italian football.

After five years of apprenticeship in Italy, enhanced by a season at Sampdoria on loan, Bruno Fernandes returned home and signed for Sporting. In Lisbon the public discovered yet another nugget of Lusitanian football. Technically sound, Fernandes had no problem in standing out, distinguishing himself in terms of assists in the Portuguese League. On the wish list of Real Madrid, the young attacking midfielder ultimately opted for the British Empire. In January 2020 for €55 million, Bruno Miguel Borges Fernandes found himself donning the famous red shirt of global behemoth Manchester United.

A five and a half year contract saw Fernandes become the sixth Portuguese player to put on the mythical Manchester United jersey. A thundering debut season was followed by goals and assists aplenty as Bruno racked up a swathe of personal awards at Old Trafford, quickly cementing himself as the heartbeat of the team and a firm fan favourite.

DID YOU KNOW?

In March 2020 during the derby against Manchester City, Bruno Fernandes crossed swords with Pep Guardiola. Both men got confused to say the least. On a throw-in the Catalan manager pretended to give him the ball back before throwing it to Luke Shaw instead. An exchange of words followed between the two protagonists before the Portuguese invited Guardiola to be silent by pointing his index finger to his mouth. United had the last laugh: they won 2–0.

FERNANDES

ARGENTINA

Enzo

FERNÁNDEZ

BORN: 17 January 2001
San Martin, Argentina

HEIGHT: 1.78 m

POSITION: Midfielder

PROFESSIONAL CAREER:
CA River Plate,
Defensa y Justicia,
Benfica, Chelsea FC

At every World Cup there's a breakout star, and in Qatar in late 2022 it was undoubtedly Enzo Fernández. The Argentine midfielder came from nowhere to win the FIFA Young Player Award following his country's triumph on football's biggest stage.

The dynamic midfielder collected his prize following, arguably, the greatest World Cup final of them all. As the post-game scene unfolded, Fernández could be forgiven for having a look of disbelief in his eyes: the 21-year-old's story is among the most remarkable in recent times. Remarkable, as Fernández only made his senior international debut in September 2022, coming on as a second-half substitute in a 3–0 friendly win over Honduras. The occasion saw Fernández fulfil a lifelong ambition to play alongside his idol, Lionel Messi.

Fernández secured his place in the squad following mature displays in two pre-tournament friendlies and having continued to excel for Portuguese club side Benfica. His rare combination of energy, perfect technique and tactical intelligence saw him swiftly acclimatise to European football following his move from boyhood club River Plate. He was a key figure for a Benfica side that swept all before them at home and abroad. The team remained unbeaten across 28 matches in all competitions and finished top of a UEFA Champions League group featuring Messi's Paris Saint-Germain.

The youngster's passing is crisp, incisive and precise, with an accuracy rate of 90 per cent in league matches in 2022 and 88 per cent during the World Cup. His ball-striking ability was memorably displayed in Argentina's do-or-die group-stage win over Mexico, when he expertly curled a shot into the top corner of Guillermo Ochoa's net to seal a 2–0 victory. He had come on as a substitute in that game but thereafter started every remaining match of Argentina's triumphant World Cup campaign.

Fernández was at his best in the showpiece final as Argentina overwhelmed France in the opening 70 minutes of the contest. Kylian Mbappé turned the game on its head as the match developed into an all-time classic, but Fernández's Argentina dug deep to eventually triumph in the most dramatic circumstances.

Having played just six months for Benfica, he was purchased by English Premier League club Chelsea in January 2023 for a British-record transfer fee.

DID YOU KNOW?

In 2016 Enzo Fernández posted an open letter on Facebook to his future teammate Lionel Messi, urging his hero to reconsider retirement from international football. 'Please don't go, Leo,' he wrote. 'Seeing you play with the light blue and white is the greatest pride in the world.' Thankfully, for Enzo and for everyone else, Messi did just that and went on to win the greatest prize of all in 2022.

ENGLAND

Phil
FODEN

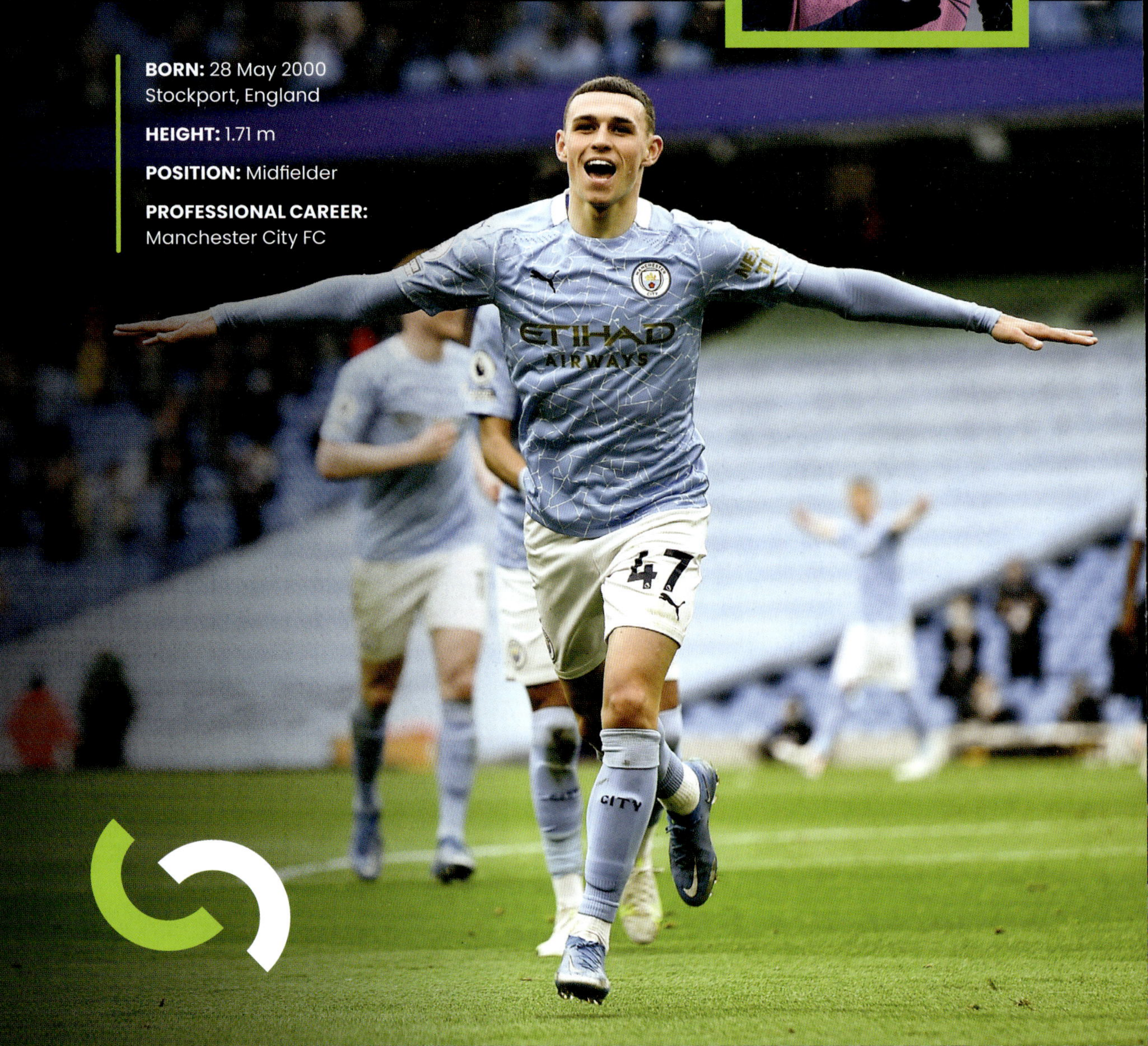

BORN: 28 May 2000
Stockport, England

HEIGHT: 1.71 m

POSITION: Midfielder

PROFESSIONAL CAREER:
Manchester City FC

DID YOU KNOW?

In December 2017 there was an appearance record for Phil Foden who, against the Ukrainians of Shakhtar Donetsk, became the youngest English player to start in a Champions League game. The previous month, at 17 years and 177 days of age, he had become the fourth youngest English player to play a European match when he replaced Yaya Touré against Feyenoord Rotterdam.

'My dad is obsessed with red, while Mum is more into sky blue,' Phil Foden said of his familial ties to Manchester's big two. Indeed, his dad is a supporter of United while his mum swears only to the Citizens. It was a tug of war that was won by Mum, little Phil preferring to follow matches at the City of Manchester Stadium, the home of City. Sitting with eyes wide open and watching on as players such as Joey Barton barked out instructions to his teammates had an effect on the young boy.

At the age of seven Foden made his first strides in the game at Reddish Vulcans, a modest Stockport club recognised for its qualities in the training of young talent. This was where Foden played his adolescent football before joining Manchester City. Joe Makin, the scout who saw his talent and recommended him to City, remembers the way Foden stood out: 'He was the shortest on the pitch,' he said, 'but you gave him the ball and all that took a back seat.'

As a ball boy at City Phil Foden scrutinised his idols of the time: James Milner, Adam Johnson, Gareth Barry and Owen Hargreaves. Foden was also passionate about the dexterous technique of a Samir Nasri or a David Silva. At the end of one match Sergio Agüero patted him on the head. Little did Phil know that four years later the Argentine international known as 'Kun' would become his teammate.

Director of football at the Citizens, the Spanish technician Txiki Begiristain encouraged Pep Guardiola to observe the phenomenon. Guardiola agreed right away that Foden was the real deal, and suddenly Foden became one of his favourite players. 'It's a gift for us and a diamond for England,' the Catalan coach raved. A rarity as an Englishman winning a starting place in the cosmopolitan make-up of the City squad, the young winger impressed with the variety of his game and his ability to read the play and create danger for opponents from all over the field.

Complemented by the quality of Kevin De Bruyne, Riyad Mahrez and latterly Erling Braut Haaland, Phil Foden has few equals. 'Every time he doesn't play I apologise to him,' Guardiola confessed as he worried about the future of his jewel, who was impatient to gain a regular spot in the star-studded City team. 'He is the only player who cannot be sold, under any circumstance. Not even for €500 million.' It appears there is no limit to what Foden is worth to his hometown team.

SPAIN

GAVI

BORN: 5 August 2004
Los Palacios y Villafranca,
Spain

HEIGHT: 1.73 m

POSITION: Central midfielder

PROFESSIONAL CAREER:
FC Barcelona

Here is the latest little genius of Spanish football. Pablo Martin Páez Gavira, better known by the nickname 'Gavi', is the new hope of La Roja, absent of such a flamboyant player since the retirement of Andrés Iniesta in the Selección midfield. At the age of 19, this is a player at ease in each of his gestures and never panicked thanks to his technical quality. The indolent Andalusian burns with pace, skill and creativity.

With incredible lucidity in his risk-taking, a disconcerting calmness on the ball and a volume of stunning games already dispatched to the archive, the darling of the Camp Nou impresses with every match played. He had only six La Liga fixtures under his belt with Barça before Luis Enrique in the fall of 2021 began calling on him to participate in the final four of the Nations League in Italy. Even more incredible is that Gavi did not even go through the usual route of youth ranks, playing barely any U-18 matches and none for the U-20.

In Milan, Italy was unable to resist the Spanish charge, Spain winning 2–1 in the semi-finals. Only France, thanks to a goal from the legendary striker Karim Benzema, were able to douse the Gavi flame. Six months later against the Czech Republic he became, at 17 years and 304 days of age, the youngest scorer in the history of the Spanish national team. The boy didn't make any noise about his personal feats, though, preferring to let his natural ability with the ball at his feet do the talking for him.

Faced with his obsession with football, dad Pablo registered Gavi at Betis Seville, close to his family, so he could satisfy his passion. In a single season Gavi scored 95 goals in the youth team, displaying his unbelievable ability at any early age. The talent of the young Andalusian quickly went beyond the borders of the south of the Iberian Peninsula. Real and Barça were already following this unique case, but it was the Catalan club that attracted the gifted eleven year old, who was invited to join the academy at La Masia, the Blaugrana training centre.

Shortly before turning 17 Gavi joined the professional team, then he was launched into the senior arena by the-then manager of Barça, Ronald Koeman. At only 18 years and 156 days, after the Basque Iker Muniain (Athletic Bilbao), Gavi became the second youngest player to reach the mark of 50 matches in La Liga. That was quicker than Leo Messi, Fernando Torres and his teammate Ansu Fati! Spanish football is reassured: without a doubt the country has her new jewel.

DID YOU KNOW?

Gavi has seen some things in his career, but he was surprised by something picked up by a young strategist. Alert to the smallest detail, an FC Barcelona coach has still not come back from it: 'Gavi has the bad habit of playing without lacing his boots!' the coach revealed. 'One day, as a joke, I asked him to show me if he knew how to tie them. He replied to me that he had not been able to do so. I told him, "One day your opponents will step on you, or you will fall!" He told me he felt more comfortable like that . . . I didn't want to upset him. Otherwise, he would no longer be Gavi!'

FRANCE

Olivier

GIROUD

BORN: 30 September 1986
Chambéry, France

HEIGHT: 1.93 m

POSITION: Striker

PROFESSIONAL CAREER:
Grenoble Foot 38, Istres, Tours FC, Montpellier HSC, Arsenal FC, Chelsea FC, AC Milan, Los Angeles FC, Lille OSC

DID YOU KNOW?

Before the Europa League final Olivier Giroud prepared an undershirt with 'Freedom in Christ' written on it to testify to his faith, but the final took place in Baku in Azerbaijan, a country with a Muslim majority. Anxious not to offend anybody, he renounced this initiative and planned to gather before the match with teammate David Luiz. Eventually, their prayer was done on the ground, knees on the floor, just after the opening of the scoring by Giroud. It was a strong moment for the hero of the match, who didn't celebrate his goal out of respect for his former team Arsenal.

He is both the second-best scorer in the history of Les Bleus and the striker who became world champion in Russia without finding the net once. That's the whole paradox of Olivier Giroud, essential to the national team but a player who has never had the unanimous backing of either coaches or fans. Criticising Giroud is even a national sport, so much so that on the eve of France versus Australia, the first match of the World Cup in Russia in 2018, there were not many people who protested his absence from the starting XI. At the end of the game the same observers who claimed his head were clamouring to see him back, because in a sluggish attack against the Socceroos the combined efforts of those selected ahead of him just weren't good enough.

Today, Giroud is an attacker who has proved his worth in some of the biggest clubs in Europe. By no means a goal-scoring machine, he is always there to create openings for others and will often find the net himself in big matches. A presence in the national team for a long time, Giroud was seen as indispensable in the eyes of Didier Deschamps. 'It's when he is not there that one realises all the importance that he has for the team,' the French coach commented.

This strong relationship was briefly undermined with the return to favour of Karim Benzema in the blue shirt and the rise and rise of Kylian Mbappé. In all the clubs he goes to, Giroud scores. While he might be less prolific than some strikers, he did finish as top scorer in the Europa League the year Chelsea won the title. Devastating in the final against his former club Arsenal, he was involved in three goals and left the Gunners regretting his release.

Upon his arrival in Italy with AC Milan he was instrumental in helping them to their 19th scudetto. His career choices allowed him to settle into the national side for a period longer than most expectations. A member of an exclusive club of players with more than 100 appearances in the national team, he overtook Thierry Henry to become France's all-time leading scorer when he netted against Poland at the 2022 World Cup in Qatar and can rightly sit alongside the greatest French internationals of all time.

Taking his unique blend of attributes to the USA and Los Angeles FC, Giroud made a shock return to Ligue Un for the new 2025–26 season, agreeing terms on a contract with Lille, where no doubt he will continue to cement his legacy.

GERMANY

Serge
GNABRY

BORN: 14 July 1995
Stuttgart, Germany

HEIGHT: 1.76 m

POSITION: Midfielder

PROFESSIONAL CAREER:
VfB Stuttgart, Arsenal FC,
West Bromwich Albion FC,
Werder Bremen,
TSG Hoffenheim,
Bayern Munich

DID YOU KNOW?

Gnabry celebrates his goals by making the gesture of turning a teaspoon in a cup. After intriguing fans of the Bundesliga, he revealed his source of inspiration. 'I am a big fan of the NBA, and especially of James Harden,' he revealed. 'The Houston Rockets point guard celebrates his decisive baskets in the money time with this small gesture, "stir the pot", which means "What's in my cup is really hot!" Like me on the field.'

It's a good idea not to annoy Serge Gnabry. During his time with Arsenal in the Premier League the talented player didn't have it all his own way and often struggled to cement a place in the Gunners starting line-up, but no matter: Serge would have his revenge, and in some style. In an unforgettable return to London in the colours of German champions Bayern Munich, Gnabry put Tottenham Hotspur to the sword, scoring four times in an incredible 7–2 victory against the team that had played the final the year before.

To register a quadruple in the Champions League is not for everyone, but to back it up a few months later with another superlative display – this time against Chelsea – was a new punishment that the English fans were not able to digest. This wasn't the Gnabry whom Chelsea had seen in the past; was it really the same player? The Gnabry that the Blues crossed paths with earlier hadn't been as mature, or as decisive or as strong.

Arriving at Arsenal as a callow youth of 16, Gnabry was introduced to the London public as the Gunners third-youngest player in Premier League history, behind only Jack Wilshere and Cesc Fàbregas. He didn't play as often in the early days, unable to make much of an impression in nine matches. An unconvincing loan at West Bromwich Albion sent him back to square one, and uncertain of his future. Even worse, he appeared to have lost the backing of manager Arsène Wenger.

The numbers didn't argue in favour of Gnabry. With the Gunners since 2012, he played only 18 games for one goal. It was clearly time for a move back to where he came from, not in his native town of Stuttgart but in a club in search of its glorious past: Werder Bremen. It was a marriage of convenience that turned into passion and allowed the career of the young German to take off.

He impressed the Bundesliga and the watching world, earning a move to Bayern Munich for €8 million and establishing himself there, ensuring life after Franck Ribéry and Arjen Robben seemed secure in Allianz Arena. A switch appeared to have been flicked and suddenly Gnabry clicked, sparking into life. At the age of 25 he had by far the best season of his career, and it's not just on the club stage that he shone.

As part of a new wind of change blowing through Die Mannschaft, Gnabry struck a memorable hat-trick on his international debut. He was the first German to achieve the feat since Dieter Muller had done so in 1976.

ENGLAND

Jack
GREALISH

BORN: 10 September 1995
Birmingham, England

HEIGHT: 1.75 m

POSITION: Midfielder

PROFESSIONAL CAREER:
Notts County FC,
Aston Villa FC,
Manchester City FC,
Everton FC (loan)

Throughout his teenage years Jack Peter Grealish sang the anthem of his country of origin – Ireland – the land of his ancestors, and he proudly wore the green jersey, but in September 2015 the Birmingham phenomenon finally chose to put on the white shirt of the Three Lions.

At the age of six he joined the academy of Aston Villa, his local club and one that has a storied history. It was a baptism of fire, a welcome to the world of football as Grealish looked to circumvent the physical challenges that inevitably came the way of the fleet-footed playmaker.

Endowed with a special technique, little Jack showed the heart of a champion. He was influenced by his Celtic heritage and played Gaelic football alongside his football training. At 16 years of age he was promoted to the Villains professional group; however, faced with severe competition, Grealish accepted a loan move to Notts County, then in League One. It wasn't long before he grabbed his first goal, in December 2013 when he dribbled past three Gillingham defenders to find the net.

A versatile player, this creator and king of improvisation can also serve as a torchbearer and provide leadership from any position across the front line, and with each touch he can dictate the tempo of the match. He has been likened to former England international Chris Waddle. A year after his maiden goal his big day came, a Premier League debut for Aston Villa, who were lined up against Manchester City. In May 2015 he progressed further, appearing for Villa in the FA Cup final, a first appearance at Wembley Stadium that ended in disappointment when Arsenal won 4–0.

Having had a taste, Grealish became more focused and celebrated a first Premier League goal in a 5–1 hammering of Norwich City in October 2019. Less than a year later, in September 2020, he made his England international debut in a 0–0 draw with Denmark. He played in the Euro 2020 final against Italy and shortly afterwards transferred to Manchester City for what was a Premier League record deal of €117 million.

After playing in the final of Euro 2020 and a much-publicised transfer to Manchester City, Grealish hoovered up plenty of silverware at the Etihad but, disillusioned about limited playing time, accepted an offer to go on loan to Everton in August 2025.

DID YOU KNOW?

You had better believe that the highest level in football is in the genes of the family of Jack Grealish: his great-great-grandfather Billy Garraty, an honourable Aston Villa striker, won the FA Cup . . . in 1905! That day, at the Crystal Palace stadium in front of more than 100,000 supporters, the flagship club of Birmingham defeated Newcastle United 2–0. And that's where his grandfather received the famous trophy.

FRANCE

Antoine
GRIEZMANN

BORN: 21 March 1991
Mâcon, France

HEIGHT: 1.76 m

POSITION: Attacker

PROFESSIONAL CAREER:
Real Sociedad,
Atlético de Madrid,
FC Barcelona, Atlético
de Madrid

Is Antoine Griezmann really French? On his ID it's clear – 'Born in Mâcon on 21 March 1991 – yet this exciting talent is a pure product of Spanish football. He failed to be spotted by clubs in his homeland, and it was in exile from the age of 13 in San Sebastian in Basque country that he was spotted by renowned talent scout Éric Olhats. Olhats became a kind of surrogate father, and under him Griezmann flourished.

Real Sociedad appreciated his technical quality, which had been rejected by a French system that was fond of big guys. Griezmann never played a single minute in a match in Ligue 1; his playground was La Liga. Forced to take his talent to a country that values the technical player, he worked on the full range of his repertoire in Pays Basque.

He began to make a name for himself under the tutelage of Philippe Montanier at Real Sociedad and exploded as a world star under the thumb of Diego Simeone at Atlético de Madrid. France did see glimpses of him, of course, during a representative career at youth level that took in France U-19s, U-20s and U-21s.

Back home the adopted Spaniard continued to pile up the goals, and in March 2014 Didier Deschamps couldn't ignore him anymore. He summoned Griezmann to the big boys and offered him his first international selection against the Netherlands. Two months later Griezmann's name was no longer a surprise when it was included in the list of 23 who would fly to Brazil for what would be Antoine's first World Cup.

In South America Antoine Griezmann began his love affair with the national team, coming to the fore under a coach who was only too happy to give him the keys to the attack. In tears following the elimination in the quarter finals against Germany, two years later he became the top scorer of Euro 2016 with six goals. That wasn't enough to pick up the title, though: France was beaten by Portugal in the final at the Stade de France.

However, 'Grizi' once again got back among the goals and in 2018 he triumphed in the Europa League, scoring a double in the final against Olympique de Marseille. Two months later he lifted the World Cup in Russia as part of a dominant French team. That year he arguably deserved the Golden Ball, but Croatian Luka Modrić was the one who was acknowledged as the king. A stint at Barcelona followed before a return to Casa Simeon and Atlético. He must have missed the Madrid air!

DID YOU KNOW?

Yet another proof of the flaws in the French training system, Antoine Griezmann fell through the cracks as a child. Although tested almost everywhere in France he never convinced, and this for one reason: his size. The main regret in the Griezmann camp was FC Metz, whose coaches had promised him a contract then retracted. 'We are not going to take your son because he is too small,' they finally admitted to Antoine's dad. Big mistake . . .

GERMANY

İlkay
GÜNDOĞAN

BORN: 24 October 1990
Gelsenkirchen, Germany

HEIGHT: 180 m

POSITION: Midfielder

PROFESSIONAL CAREER:
FC Nürnberg,
Borussia Dortmund,
Manchester City FC,
FC Barcelona,
Manchester City FC,
Galatasaray SK

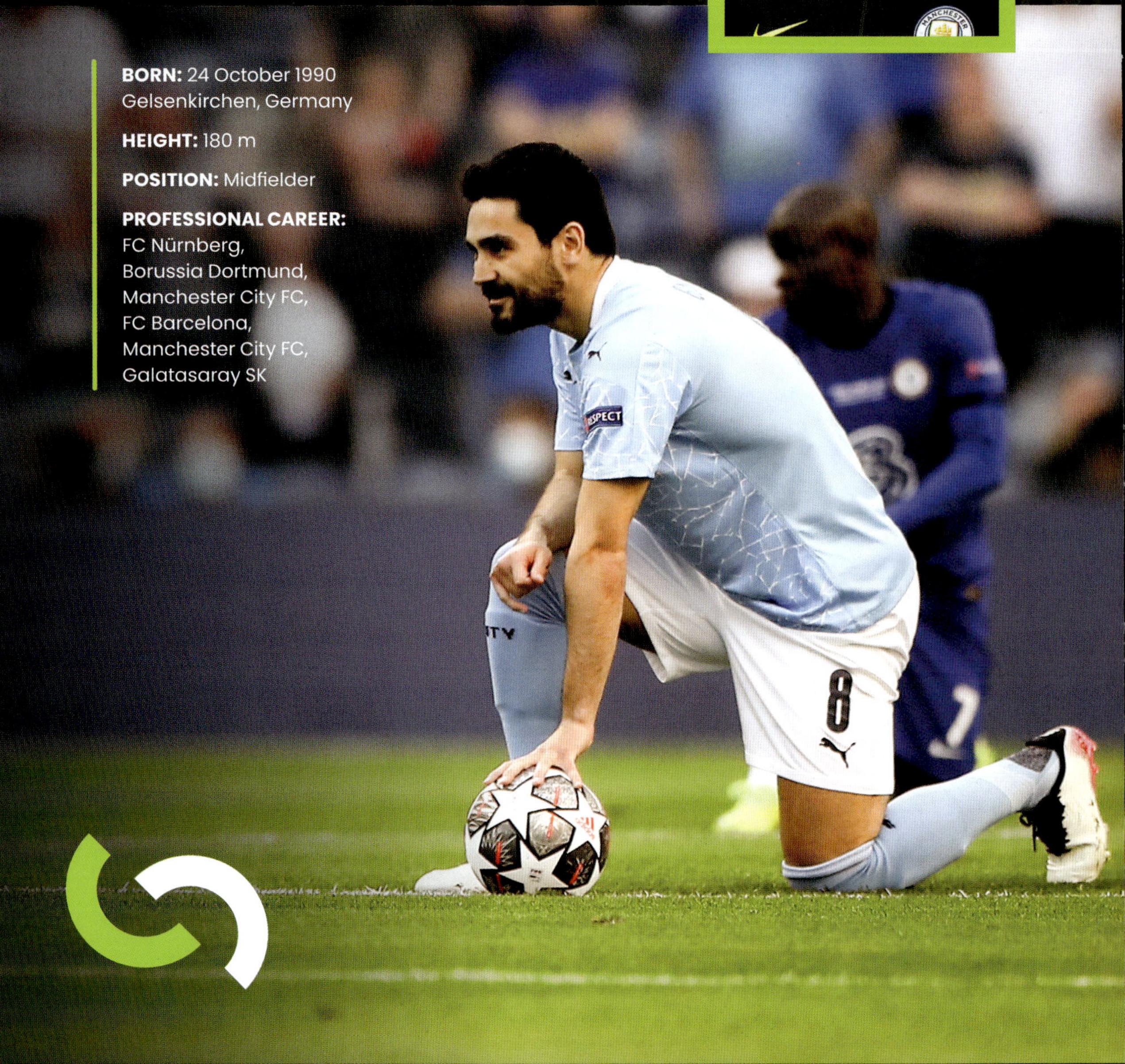

The spine is vital, and especially for an athlete at the highest level. İlkay Gündoğan learned this the hard way in the autumn of 2012. During an international break, he landed badly and spent a night in hell; a subsequent MRI revealed a root infection in the nerves in his vertebrae. This was a hammer blow for this piston of the midfield who, at only 22 years of age, suffered atrociously.

To everyone's surprise he left for treatment in the Crimea, near Ukraine. 'My volleyball player cousin suffered from the same injury. She was well cared for there,' was the justification of the German international of Turkish origin. Coming from Gelsenkirchen in the middle of the Ruhr, he logically performed his first steps on the grass at Schalke 04, the big local club. As a teenager he joined his half-brother Paul Johar at VfL Bochum to complete his training.

By then İlkay had earned a reputation as a playmaker across the Rhine. An innately talented one, he created opportunities and distributed wonderfully, a purveyor of sumptuous passing benefiting from a panoramic view and a unique sense of tempo. In short, he was the hub of his team. Some considered him slow at this stage, but his massive importance to the team meant that his coach at Borussia Dortmund, Jürgen Klopp, considered him vital and hatched a plan to get the best from his technician.

Klopp slowed the tempo of the performance a notch and made Gündoğan a relay in the centre of the park, a position for which he is now renowned. In the latter months of 2011 Joachim Löw in turn cracked the code and selected Gündoğan within the Nationalmannschaft for the first time.

After five seasons on the banks of the Rhine, in June 2016 Gündoğan opted for Manchester City FC. It was a good deal for the Sky Blues and for Pep Guardiola, who enlisted one of the best specialists of his position on the continent for only €25 million. 'He is so smart that he understands the game perfectly,' Guardiola insisted. 'He knows in every action what is the best for the group.' Installed at the Citizens, the cerebral German has a bright future ahead of him if his back leaves him in peace. Gündoğan departed City for FC Barcelona in 2023–24 before making a swift return a season later. After another exceptional year he finally left for good, signing for Turkish giants Galatasaray.

DID YOU KNOW?

The thunderbolt triggered in May 2021 by the giants of European football, all eager to create a Super League, was little denounced by its main actors. The footballers were discreet – except İlkay Gündoğan, one of the few to speak about this project. 'Some always want more matches. Anyone thinking of us players?' he asked. 'The current Champions League format works very well and that's why it's popular.'

SWEDEN

Viktor

GYÖKERES

BORN: : 4 June 1998,
Stockholm, Sweden

HEIGHT: 1.89 m

POSITION: Striker

PROFESSIONAL CAREER:
IF Brommapojkarna,
Brighton & Hove Abion FC,
FC St Pauli (loan),
Swansea City AFC (loan),
Coventry City (loan),
Coventry City FC,
Sporting CP, Arsenal FC

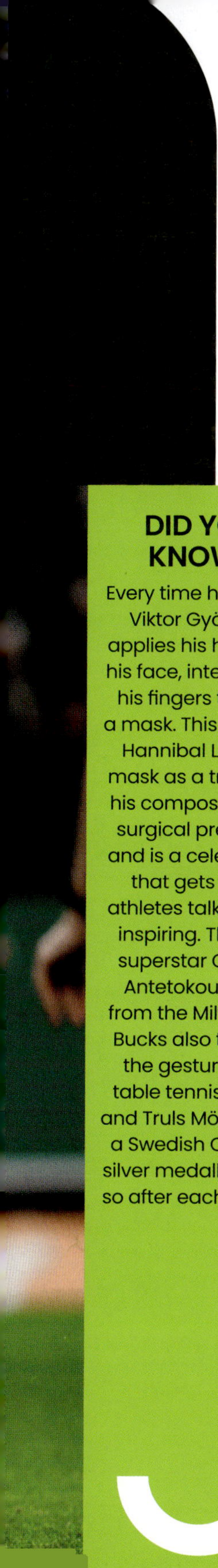

Viktor Gyökeres entered the field as someone enters a scrum: without manners, shoulders outstretched, ready for anything. He is the kind of guy who takes the space, the ball and morale and gives nothing away and is a striker in the almost animal sense of the term: big, solid and not necessarily elegant but supremely efficient.

Trained at Brommapojkarna, the Stockholm factory club, Viktor made his professional debut at the age of 17 and was quick to get noticed. 'I've always had this obsession to finish off the play. It doesn't matter how it happens, I just want to finish it.' Brighton was quick to spot him, but as is often the case in England he remained stuck in the B Team and unable to make the breakthrough. This was nothing serious, though, as Viktor was learning.

At Swansea and then Coventry he discovered the harshness of British football with scraped knees and hard duels, and he thrived on them. It was at Coventry that he exploded, with 21 goals in the championship and a rare ability to influence nearly every game he played in. This form aroused the interest of clubs in mainland Europe.

Sporting Lisbon attracted him the most, and for €20 million the Portuguese club got their man. An incredible haul of 97 goals in 102 matches followed, repaying the fee many times over. This striker rate made the biggest clubs pay attention and in the summer of 2025 Arsenal managed to claim his signature, paying a fee of €54.8 million, plus an additional €8.6 million in add-ons.

Gyökeres doesn't have a conventional style but rather his own way of playing. He doesn't dribble to please: he dribbles to kill, with his size and the torso of a wrestler hiding a feline speed. He likes to start his runs from deep, devour spaces and rush headlong into the action. The kind of player who doesn't let his opponent breathe, either in the air or on the ground.

In Sweden he is compared with Zlatan Ibrahimović for his origin and quiet arrogance. In reality he is closer to an alternative Haaland: less robotic, more raw, not so much a star but just as obsessed with scoring goals. In the national team, for whom he made his debut in 2019 against Finland, he is starting to take over as the leading man. With the shade of Ibra finally dissipated, Gyökeres is the new spearhead of the blågult. Not talkative, Viktor prefers to let his feet and especially his shoulders do the talking, his physical prowess a leading part of his game. Portuguese defenders will no doubt attest to his impressive physicality.

DID YOU KNOW?

Every time he scores Viktor Gyökeres applies his hands to his face, intertwining his fingers to form a mask. This imitates Hannibal Lecter's mask as a tribute to his composure and surgical precision, and is a celebration that gets other athletes talking and inspiring. The NBA superstar Giannis Antetokounmpo from the Milwaukee Bucks also took up the gesture, and table tennis player and Truls Möregårdh, a Swedish Olympic silver medallist, does so after each victory.

NORWAY

Erling Braut
HAALAND

BORN: 21 July 2000
Leeds, England

HEIGHT: 1.94 m

POSITION: Striker

PROFESSIONAL CAREER:
Bryne FK, Molde FK,
FC Red Bull Salzbourg,
Borussia Dortmund,
Manchester City FC

DID YOU KNOW?

A fervent practitioner of meditation, Erling Braut Haaland regularly indulges in yoga. It is from this discipline that he draws his celebration when he scores: he sits, legs crossed and hands open, in the posture called siddhasana. During the U-20 World Cup in May 2019 he might well have abused this use after plundering nine goals against Honduras, with the young Norwegians recording an astonishing 12–0 victory.

Faced with the infernal growth curve of the young man the medical staff from Molde, the Norwegian club where Erling Braut Haaland played, put him on enforced rest. The future star was then only 17 years old but already had tremendous potential. All the more atypical was that the chubby-faced Viking grew up in the United Kingdom, where his father, Alf-Inge Haaland, was a professional footballer from Nottingham Forest to Manchester City via Leeds United, where the future sharpshooter had been born.

On the pitch the young starlet began playing with adults from the age of 15, lining up for Bryne FK during a modest cup match in Norway. He had a trial in Germany at Hoffenheim, but the leaders of the Baden-Württemberg side denied him a contract because the demands of one were outside their usual pay scale. Thus Haaland started in the professional ranks on 1 February 2017 with Molde, his protective club that was then being trained by Ole Gunnar Solskjær, the future Manchester United manager. In August 2018 he was recruited by Red Bull Salzburg, but he did not land in Austria until six months later. That was the beginning of the explosion of this prodigy.

Everything really clicked when the season resumed in the autumn of 2019. Under the prism of the Champions League the public discovered the Norwegian machine whose quickdraw shooting, pace and silky touch were allied with an impressive physique that dominated defenders. In half a dozen Champions League group matches Haaland slammed in eight goals, including a hat-trick in his first match against KRC Genk that was won 6–2. He also found the net against Liverpool and Napoli.

In the Austrian championship the Norwegian Gulliver scored more goals (29) than he had played matches (27). In December 2019 Borussia Dortmund took a chance on the phenomenon, and in his first game in the Bundesliga on 18 January 2020 he began to repay them. Brought on in the 56th minute as the Schwarzgelben trailed FC Augsburg 1–3, a 26-minute hat-trick gave Dortmund a remarkable 5–3 win.

A City fan since early childhood, the new Sky Blues striker joined Guardiola at the club in 2022 and hit the ground running amid a blaze of goals and a swathe of hat-tricks. The Norwegian hitman broke record after record in his Premier League debut season, scoring 52 goals as Manchester City claimed the treble of Premier League, FA Cup and the Holy Grail of the UEFA Champions League.

MOROCCO

Achraf

HAKIMI

BORN: 4 November 1998
Madrid, Spain

HEIGHT: 1.81 m

POSITION: Defender

PROFESSIONAL CAREER:
Real Madrid,
Borussia Dortmund,
Inter Milan,
Paris Saint-Germain FC

Being trained at Real Madrid is not a guarantee for a place under the sun. The Merengues club stacks the ranks with stars and imports far more players than they tend to promote through the youth ranks. Achraf Hakimi started his journey from slightly further afar: born in Morocco, he moved to Getafe in the Madrid suburbs when his parents took the family from North Africa to Spain. His undoubted talent saw the door of the Real Madrid training institute open to him at just seven years of age.

Hakimi's model was a hairy Brazilian with a Portuguese accent and fantastic runs up and down the left channel. He had Marcelo as his idol early on and dreamed of the day he might evolve enough to play alongside him. Shy and persevering, the Moroccan believed in his lucky star and refused to go and see if the grass was greener elsewhere. If it was going to be hard to break through well, so be it.

He hoped to catch the eye of head coach Zinedine Zidane, who was never afraid to take a look into the Madrid nursery and see what rough demands could be taken and polished. Hakimi lacked neither guts nor talent. He quickened the pace of his acceleration as he was eager to progress alongside his training partners, who were all patiently waiting for their turn to shine. Climbing the ladder at a rapid rate, the Hispano-Moroccan found himself doing summer preparations with the professionals even though he was not then old enough to drive a car.

With pace and technique Hakimi's attacking style seduced Zidane, and the Madridista coach did not hesitate to call him for training with Ronaldo and gang before throwing him into the deep end at 19 years of age. A plethora of injuries to those in front of him saw Hakimi burst from almost complete anonymity to holder of the right-back position. In the process he became the first Moroccan to wear the Real Madrid shirt in an official match, then he scored his first professional goal on the Bernabéu pitch after a strike was created by Karim Benzema.

He became the first Atlas Lion to lift the big-eared cup as Real conquered Europe again. However, the fall was to be brutal. Zidane's surprise departure from Real did not help Achraf, and his status as a regular starter did little to resist the return of the Madrid wounded. Borussia Dortmund sniffed an opportunity and took the player on loan before he was transferred to Inter Milan, then he made a move to France with Paris Saint-Germain in 2021.

DID YOU KNOW?

When Real Madrid was looking for a way out for its young player in 2018, Olympique de Marseille (OM) inquired about Hakimi's availability. The sports director at the time, Andoni Zubizarreta, led the first approach but the proposed deal was quickly abandoned. Achraf was perceived to be too young and not physical enough for Ligue 1. Finally, he joined Dortmund in the Bundesliga as one of the best in the world at his job and is now out of the price range for OM. It is their rival, PSG, who have him on the roster.

GERMANY

Kai

HAVERTZ

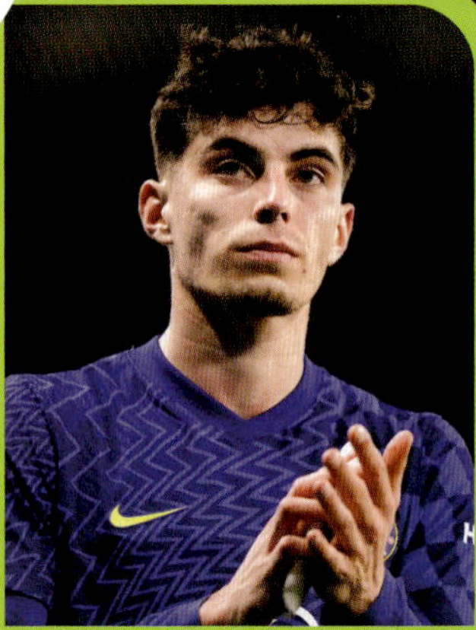

BORN: 11 June 1999
Aachen, Germany

HEIGHT: 1.90 m

POSITION: Attacker

PROFESSIONAL CAREER:
Bayer 04 Leverkusen,
Chelsea FC, Arsenal FC

DID YOU KNOW?

If it was with his grandfather Richard that Kai touched his first footballs, it was with his big brother that he got a taste of music. Guitar for the eldest, Kai played his first notes on his grandmother's piano and caught the music virus. He continues in his free time to play his favourite melodies, as it is a way to decompress and avoid false notes in his career.

In the midst of a health and financial crisis, most of the leaders of European football thought twice before splurging in the transfer market – but there is always an exception to the rule. The club that did the breaking was Chelsea, and the person involved was Kai Havertz. The Blues did not dither in their pursuit of the promising German, who had already been making waves in his homeland. The youngest player to pull on the shirt of Bayer 04 Leverkusen in the Bundesliga, at the age of 17 and 126 days, his performances quickly earned admirers from beyond the German borders.

Tall, technical and with excellent vision, Havertz can do it all. The price of the phenomenon raised eyebrows, Chelsea happily paying the €80 million requested by Bayer Leverkusen for this 21-year-old international. Whether this would prove valuable – well, the future soon told us it would.

The stage was the Estádio do Dragão in Porto in the final of the 2021 Champions League. At the tail end of the first half Havertz was played in by Mason Mount and, faced with Ederson advancing in the Manchester City goal, did not hesitate, slipping the ball into the net for what was to be the match-winning goal. It had taken some time for Havertz to register his first goal, but he instantly became the unexpected hero of the Blues as Chelsea won the European Cup for only the second time in their history.

It was a spectacular happy ending in what had been a particularly difficult season for Kai Havertz. Taxed as the most expensive player of the summer transfer window in 2020 the expectation was enormous, and each appearance was closely scrutinised. Indeed, he was persistently reminded of his transfer fee throughout the season, something the German shrugged off. 'Obviously it's a big transfer, but I think it's normal in football at the present time to spend such sums,' Havertz said. 'So, it does not put me under too much pressure, because I don't play well or badly because of the price of my transfer.'

The arrival of compatriot Thomas Tuchel on the manager's bench to replace Frank Lampard kick-started Havertz's campaign. Like the whole team, Havertz metamorphosed and gradually returned to the starting XI before scoring the famous goal in the final against City as a regular. 'Havertz has qualities,' Tuchel commented. 'He needs to show them. It's that simple!' Havertz ruffled a few feathers in London by switching blue for red in 2023–24, signing for Arsenal.

FRANCE

Lucas

HERNANDEZ

BORN: 14 February 1996
Marseille, France

HEIGHT: 1.84 m

POSITION: Defender

PROFESSIONAL CAREER:
Atlético de Madrid,
Bayern Munich,
Paris Saint-Germain FC

DID YOU KNOW?

Lucas Hernandez's brother Théo was, like him, born in Marseille and trained at Atlético. Loaned to Real Sociedad in 2018, the cadet also evolved to the left-side position. A former defender at Toulouse and Sochaux-Montbéliard and then at Marseille, their father, Jean-François Hernandez, also played in La Liga for Compostela, Rayo Vallecano and Atlético between 1998 and 2002. In the grip of serious financial difficulties, the father fled Spain in 2004 without leaving an address and all trace of him was lost in Thailand.

It is the surprise guest who does not skimp on small gifts that are most welcomed and adopted by their hosts. Three months away from the 2018 World Cup in Russia, with Benjamin Mendy having been freshly operated on and the cruciate ligament of his right knee requiring treatment, talk involved who would replace him on Les Bleus left flank. The names Layvin Kurzawa, Lucas Digne and Jordan Amavi were mentioned, each having their backers.

Someone who wasn't in the conversation was Lucas Hernandez. His entry into the squad, at the Stade De France in a 2–3 loss to Colombia in March 2018, allowed the young man from Madrid to show his potential to the French public. 'Loukass' really had nothing to lose in selection and, without pressure, he blended into the tricolour group and seduced his coach.

Didier Deschamps had persuaded him a few weeks earlier to join the France group, but above all urged him not to follow up on his wishes to respond to the invitation of the Iberian Federation.

'When I say that Spain gave me everything, personally and professionally, it is a truth,' the native of Marseilles insisted. 'I spent my entire football career there until then. Not excluding the fact that I speak better Spanish, but that does not prevent my country from being France!' Capped, the adopted Castilian didn't leave the line-up, and from his sensational debut he scaled the heights. His country landed the supreme title in Moscow in only his 12th international match!

Hernandez is a relentless trainer: Deschamps was just one coach who appreciated his intense approach to sessions. The left side of Atlético has a vice that is appreciated by the boss of the Blues and by his deputy, Guy Stéphan. With such a pit bull in the ranks, defensive guarantees are assured.

Trained and forged in the hard school of the Colchoneros, Lucas Hernandez demonstrated mental and tactical discipline that was well above average at a young age. When selecting their best XI from those who played in La Liga, the experts were almost unanimous in picking Hernandez for the left-sided defensive berth, and in the summer of 2019 when he arrived at Bayern Munich it was with the strong esteem of the German public. With such qualities, Lucas appears to be a long-term solution for his country, while he has since swapped the Bavarian giants for Paris and PSG.

FRANCE

Théo HERNANDEZ

BORN: 6 October 1997
Marseille, France

HEIGHT: 1.84 m

POSITION: Defender

PROFESSIONAL CAREER:
Atlético de Madrid,
Alavés, Real Madrid,
Real Sociedad, AC Milan,
Al Hilal SFC

One Hernandez can hide another! Do you know Lucas? Then you will love Théo: the same aggressiveness, the same thirst for victory and the same blue jersey with the rooster on the chest. Théo Hernandez walks in the footsteps of his older brother, and it's not uncommon for the French national team defence to be 50 per cent populated by the same family. Nothing seems to resist the young talent; you only need to ask the supporters of the Rossoneri to understand the esteem in which the AC Milan left back is held.

Indisputable and essential alongside the likes of Zlatan Ibrahimović and the local Italian stars, Theo's cannon shots and defensive nous allowed the former club of Silvio Berlusconi to regain its lost glory. Theo takes on all obstacles and everything that revolves around them and more often than not comes out on top. Currently, everything is going pretty well for him. It is often when he is on vacation in Spain that the career of the youngest Hernandez does go awry.

The first time was in June 2017 on the Costa del Sol in Marbella. Théo was enjoying the sun and the beaches at the Rally of Hopes rather than attending France U-21 training under Sylvain Ripoll. 'I did a mistake of youth,' Hernandez said. 'I will also say that I was not pushed to go, which some people may have hoped, but that I chose Spain. There was my transfer to Real Madrid, which I was negotiating at that time. That, more that, more that . . . But I made an error.'

Théo admitted the stupidity of his act and was quickly forgiven, and the second time was a little more glorious. The scene took place in the heat of Ibiza at an appointment with a legend, Paolo Maldini, the current technical director of Milan. It changed everything, albeit in a good way this time. Everything was accelerating, and Théo signed for the Italians and soon settled as a starter in the Milan rearguard.

Beyond his achievements, which a good accountant would struggle to keep tally of, his pace, technique and athletic qualities make him an essential cog of Stefano Pioli's XI. His ability to run all day, both in defensive coverage and on offensive surges and especially in the last minutes of matches, impressed everyone. Of course, this praise has been rained freely on the native of Marseille, who had made a place for himself in Serie A. A shift to a new club came in 2025–26 when Hernandez headed to Al Hilal.

DID YOU KNOW?

The presentation to the public is a moment known to impress the eyes of the club's fans, but it can also prove embarrassing if the technique is not there. Ex-Real Madrid left back Théo Hernandez made it a bitter experience: officially presented at the Santiago Bernabéu stadium, the young Frenchman indulged in the traditional photo session in front of the press before doing some juggling but, alas, it didn't go as planned. Théo was embarrassed to manage just six juggles, a failure that fortunately was without consequences for the future.

AUSTRALIA

Nestory

IRANKUNDA

BORN: 9 February 2006, Kigoma, Tanzania

HEIGHT: 1.75 m

POSITION: Winger

PROFESSIONAL CAREER: Adelaide Croatia Raiders, Adelaide United FC, Bayern Munich, Grasshopper Club Zurich (loan), Watford FC

DID YOU KNOW?

Nestory moved to Australia, arriving in Perth when he was just three months old. His parents, originally from war-torn Burundi where a civil war was threatening to tear the country apart, had fled their homeland to a refugee camp in Tanzania and it was there, in Kigoma, that Irankunda was born. The youngster was surrounded by love in a large family of eight children, with two older brothers and five younger sisters.

With a couple of swings of his right foot, Australian winger Nestory Irankunda introduced himself to his new supporters of the Hornets, Watford FC. The sprightly set-piece expert curled home two superlative free kicks within the space of a week to loud acclaim, both in the United Kingdom and back home in his native land. For those who had watched his progress it came as little surprise.

From the moment he set foot on a football pitch as a young hopeful with Northern Wolves and Parafield Guardians, Irankunda's energy, work rate and ability to manipulate a ball were evident. His talent was spotted at the latter club and he was scouted by Adelaide Croatia Raiders, where he was a standout in their youth teams. That meant that the local A-League team, Adelaide United, became interested in this prodigy and he signed terms in 2021.

Initially playing with the youth set-up in the National Premier League, Irankunda was magnificent so it was only a matter of time before he was promoted to the senior squad. That happened at the age of 15 years and 333 days, with Irankunda becoming the sixth youngest player in A-League history when he debuted for the Reds against Melbourne Victory.

A first goal followed shortly after, against the Newcastle Jets, but it was the following season that was his breakthrough year. A series of excellent performances and some incredible strikes over the next two years, including a first professional hat-trick against Western United, alerted the scouts of clubs from overseas and a move to Europe beckoned.

The German goliath Bayern Munich secured his signature, with the talented player being named as an unused substitute in the early months of his contract. Irankunda found it tough to break into the Munich first team, which is no easy feat, so a loan spell with Grasshoppers in the Swiss Super League followed. Watford were impressed by what they saw, and the English championship club signed him in 2025.

At international level fans had been clamouring to see Irankunda in a national team shirt, and they got their wish in 2024 when he was handed a debut in a FIFA World Cup qualifier against Bangladesh. He scored his first international goal a few days later against Palestine from the penalty spot, becoming the second-youngest goal scorer for the national team.

BRAZIL

Gabriel

JESUS

BORN: 3 April 1997
São Paulo, Brazil

HEIGHT: 1.75 m

POSITION: Forward

PROFESSIONAL CAREER:
SE Palmeiras,
Manchester City FC,
Arsenal FC

DID YOU KNOW?

In September 2014, while 17-year-old Gabriel Jesus had not then played professionally, he was offered to Olympique Lyonnais (OL) by Marcelo, a talent scout for President Aulas in Brazil. 'I had indicated this young player to Florian Maurice [the OL scout]. I had also sent videos to the coaches and owners, and at the time he could have left Palmeiras for less than €1 million. But they did not respond. Then it exploded and it was too late!'

No one had imagined such a trajectory for a kid who grew up in a derelict district in the north of the megalopolis of São Paulo, more precisely in Jardim Peri. The young Brazilian had to fight to stand out from the very beginning. Raised with his three brothers by his widowed mother, little Gabriel Fernando de Jesus suffered from the absence of a father. On the pitch and despite his precocious ease with the ball, he passed through the football mesh unnoticed.

The teenager was even playing in defence when he put on the green and white jersey of the modest Pequeninos do Meio Ambiente. At the age of 15, when future professionals are already on the circuit being groomed for stardom, Gabriel evolved with the Associação Atlética Anhanguera and was noticed by a Palmeiras scout. A conclusive test soon followed when he donned the famous jersey of the great Paulista club, created more than a century ago by Italian migrants.

'Like everyone, I was first struck by its speed,' Bruno Petri, his trainer at the club, recalled. 'Above all, he had one more thing: he was determined.' Gabriel was aware that he had fallen behind others, so he worked harder. In Brazil he was called a 'white fly', a player who has had an atypical career. As if by chance, upon his induction into the cutting edge of the first team Palmeiras won the national title that had eluded them for 22 years. With 12 goals in 27 matches and voted best player in the Brazilian championship, Gabriel became the hero of the green people.

In a few months he put aside all the shortcomings in his game: his tactics, heading game and deficiencies were a thing of the past. Even the elders at Palmeiras were impressed by the little genius, and they weren't the only ones. Manchester United, Barcelona, Real Madrid, Bayern Munich and Paris Saint-Germain were all on the hunt for the Paulista pearl.

However, a phone call to the player from Pep Guardiola in the summer of 2016 made the difference. While Gabriel led the Seleção to the Olympic title during the Rio Olympics, he agreed to join Manchester City. Doubts were quickly swept away, and despite some physical hiccups the young Brazilian exploded in dynamite mode with the Citizens then continued on in that same vein upon transferring to north London giants Arsenal.

BRAZIL

Vinícius

JÚNIOR

BORN: 12 July 2000
Sao Goncalo, Brazil

HEIGHT: 1.76 m

POSITION: Winger

PROFESSIONAL CAREER:
Flamengo, Real Madrid

Just crowned world champion for the second time in his career, Ronaldo (the real one!) arrived in Madrid, where Florentino Pérez did not hesitate to drop €45 million to ease him from the grasp of Inter Milan. Nearly 16 years later it was in the guise of the godfather that Ronaldo trod the lush green grass of the Santiago-Bernabéu Stadium again, this time to accompany 18-year-old Vinícius Júnior, who had arrived from Brazilian side Flamengo.

The Brazilian left winger may have cost the same sum as his companion – €45 million – but the spectators did not rush to attend his little session of juggling that day. However, with his label as the seventh-most expensive player in the history of the Merengues and the second-most expensive La Liga transfer in the summer of 2018, behind Thomas Lemar at Atlético,

Vinícius Júnior could expect the red carpet to be rolled out for him. But, no! Adored at the Maracanã Stadium in Rio in the jersey of Flamengo, he found himself playing matches with Castilla. The Spanish third division was a baptism of fire in European football, and daily life was not as glamorous as he imagined it would be when he left Rio de Janeiro. 'Vini Jr', though, proved himself with Castilla and ended up sitting on the bench facing Getafe to get a closer look at the band of Benzema.

Appearances were fleeting, but the Brazilian winger did not get impatient and decided not to use a clause in his contract that would have allowed him to return on loan from January 2019 to Flamengo if his position on the bench continued. A move back then might have signalled the end of his dream with the Merengues, especially since a certain Rodrygo Goes, a 17-year-old left winger nicknamed the 'new Neymar', was supposed to arrive from Santos, from where he was bought for, ironically, €45 million.

Time was running out for Vinícius Júnior, but he seized his chance when it was given to him and put in some formidable performances. However, an injury slowed his progress. Victim of a rupture of the tibia-fibula joint in the right ankle in a Champions League match against Ajax Amsterdam, he came back faster than expected in training but was ultimately not selected for the Copa América alongside his great idol Neymar. They have already rubbed shoulders within the Brazilian national selection; how long before they are reunited at club level?

DID YOU KNOW?

In Vinícius Júnior's case Manchester United had a head start on the transfer of the Brazilian nugget, but the South American did not immediately tread the grass of the Theatre of Dreams. This was the fault of the chief executive of United, Ed Woodward, who procrastinated over the deal. Discussions dragged on and allowed Barcelona and Real Madrid to enter the race for his signature. In the end, Madrid won the day.

ENGLAND

Harry KANE

BORN: 28 July 1993
Walthamstow, England

HEIGHT: 1.88 m

POSITION: Striker

PROFESSIONAL CAREER:
Tottenham Hotspur FC,
Leyton Orient, Millwall FC,
Norwich City,
Leicester City FC,
Tottenham Hotspur FC,
Bayern Munich

DID YOU KNOW?

The Tottenham hero previously wore the kit of Spurs's sworn enemy, Arsenal FC. Harry Kane played for the North London rival's club academy in 2001–02 as an eight year old, having joined them from his local side Ridgeway Rovers. His time with the Gunners was short lived, with Arsenal releasing him after a year. He went on to sign with Tottenham in 2004, the club he supported as a child.

Harry Kane has been central to England's trophy hunt since 2015, first captaining his national side two years later. His 2018 form saw him finish that year's World Cup as the tournament's top scorer, finding the back of the net six times in Russia. He then became the UEFA's top scorer in both the 2020 European and 2022 World Cup qualifiers, scoring 12 goals in each. His performances during Euro 2020, which included four goals, saw him lead England to their first major final since 1966.

This cursory glance at Kane's recent successes makes it hard to believe there was a time with the Three Lions when the striker struggled with his form. Arguably, being Wayne Rooney's successor was never going to be an easy task. Prior to being named England's 119th captain in 2017 Kane had encountered a 12-month goal drought. You can only be impressed by the mental strength and fortitude it took for him to turn struggle into success.

This was not new to Kane, though. Nicknamed 'Hurrykane' by English supporters due to his exploits at Wembley, the striker had started his career as the butt of their jokes. During his adolescence, everything from his accent to his physicality drew criticism. Encumbered by his height, the young player appeared too slow, too scrawny and lacking in tactical ability. To put it bluntly, his ability to ever be able to compete in the Premier League was questioned.

Sceptical coaches at Tottenham's football academy repeatedly sent out the young Kane on loan, hoping the discreet and ungainly teenager could progress. Starting out at Brisbane Road with League One's Leyton Orient, he then ventured to The Den to play for cut-throat Championship side Millwall FC. This was followed by spells at Norwich and Leicester City, each step seeing the Londoner gain in skill and confidence as he put his body on the line in front of hostile crowds.

Years later Kane spoke of the impact of his time on loan, specifically with Millwall. 'I was 18, we were in a relegation battle and it turned me into a man. I played in difficult, high-pressure games and I managed to come out of it positively.'

The summer of 2023 saw Kane at the centre of a transfer saga that captivated the world. Having given Tottenham Hotspur his all, breaking the club goal-scoring record, Kane was a wanted man. Eventually, it was German giants Bayern Munich who snagged the number 9, the Bavarians reaping the rewards of a sensational start to life in Germany for England's skipper, who began his German career in a blizzard of goals.

FRANCE

N'Golo
KANTÉ

BORN: 29 March 1991
Paris, France

HEIGHT: 1.68 m

POSITION: Midfielder

PROFESSIONAL CAREER:
US Boulogne CO,
Stade Malherbe Caen,
Leicester City FC,
Chelsea FC, Al-Ittihad

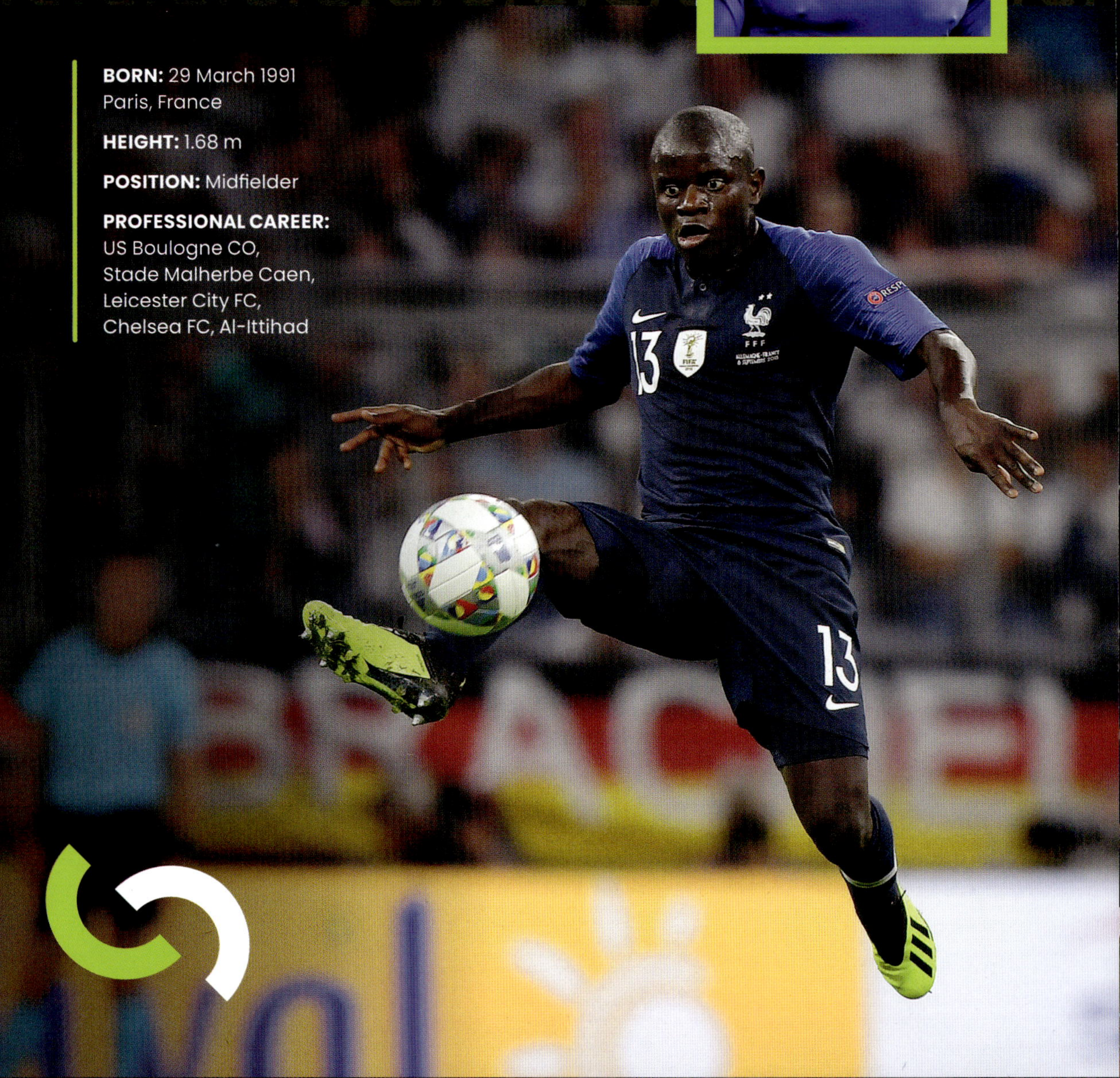

DID YOU KNOW?

Born in Paris to Malian parents, N'Golo Kanté could have played for the Mali Eagles. However, he ended up representing France, making his debut in 2016 against the Netherlands. Two years later he was a World Cup champion.

French head coach Didier Deschamps was bitterly disappointed upon hearing the news that his midfield talisman would miss the 2022 FIFA World Cup due to injury. A mainstay in France's starting line-up for half a decade, the diminutive player's absence was a blow to Les Bleus because N'Golo Kanté is a paradox, being unavoidable and indefensible on the field while remaining completely modest and shy off it. As a man he garners respect; as a player he shines. His work rate, defensive plays, attacking creativity and tactical knowhow always betters the team as a collective. Said simply, he is an overall top bloke and good teammate.

From a young age Kanté often played up age levels. While most predicted a career as a professional, he originally struggled to find a place at a football academy: 'too small' was a comment often used by scouts and recruiters. It wasn't until the age of 21, when he played for French Ligue 2 side Boulogne-sur-Mer, that his exploits started to draw attention. He then moved to fellow Ligue 2 side Caen, where his game went to another level.

He participated in the promotion of his new side to Ligue 1, where he joined the elite of French football. This introduction quickly made him the revelation of the 2014–15 season and led to his multi-million euro recruitment by Leicester City. His first season in England became a fairytale, his new English club stunning the football world by winning the Premier League – in part due to Kanté's contribution. Creative, fast and dynamic, N'Golo dazzled. 'One day, I'm going to see him cross the ball, and then finish the cross with a header himself,' his head coach, Claudio Ranieri, stated.

Chelsea FC bought Kanté at the end of the season and won the Premier League a year later. Former England international and pundit Gary Lineker tweeted: 'Leicester with Kanté: Champions. Without Kanté: struggling. Chelsea last season: struggled. With Kanté: top. Coincidence? I don't think so.'

Kanté won the PFA Players' Player of the Year. His individual and collective achievements continued with Chelsea, from two FIFA FIFPro World 11 appearances to the UEFA Europa League and Champions League and the highest prize: the World Cup. There is one thing that Kanté has not shied away from and that is winning trophies, which he aims to continue at new employees Al-Ittihad in the Saudi Pro League.

GERMANY

Joshua KIMMICH

BORN: 8 February 1995
Rottweil, Germany

HEIGHT: 1.76 m

POSITION: Midfielder

PROFESSIONAL CAREER:
VfB Stuttgart, RB Leipzig, Bayern Munich

KIMMICH

If you were asked to nominate a German footballer with stereotypical metronome qualities you need not look further than Joshua Kimmich. The Bayern man has evolved into a perfect balance between attack and defence and is one of the best number 6s around. With his tactical intelligence, versatility in the middle of the pitch and utility as a right back during Pep Guardiola's stint with the Bavarian side, Kimmich has long been the beating midfield heart of both Munich and Germany's squads. Confident and strong, 'Jo' is known for his mental resilience and capacity to motivate the sides he plays in, with style to match.

This style can be traced to Rottweil, between the Black Forest and bourgeois Stuttgart and Kimmich's parents' garden, to be precise. The problem, though, was young Jo's destruction of his parents' backyard while bouncing the football off a wall. A move to the local amateur football club, and an instruction to play at the end of the laneway if itching for a kick with his friends at home, started a journey that led to the game's highest levels.

Kimmich trained first with Bösingen. He then moved to the Bundesliga side of VfB Stuttgart's academy. The teenager continued to develop there and slowly built his skills, but he never signed with the top-flight German side. One of his coaches even told the youngster, 'You are not good enough, your body is not strong enough.' It was with third-division side RB Leipzig that Jo signed in the summer of 2013.

He moved to Bundesliga giants Bayern Munich ahead of the 2015–16 season and never looked back. Consistent performances during his first season combined with a double trophy win – the DFB-Pokal and Bundesliga – saw the young player called up to the national team's 2016 European campaign in France. In 2017 he became the Mannschaft's youngest captain.

After Germany's disastrous exit at the 2022 FIFA Men's World Cup, when Kimmich said he was afraid he'd fall into a hole few doubted his resolve to drag his national side to the pinnacle of international football.

DID YOU KNOW?

When Joshua Kimmich's transfer to Bayern Munich was being discussed in the summer of 2015, the Bavarian club dragged its feet. A higher up in the Munich establishment was unconvinced by the young Rottweiler. German football legend Karl-Heinz Rummenigge was sceptical about the young German yet Kimmich turned out to be a bargain, costing Bayern less than €10 million.

FRANCE

Presnel
KIMPEMBE

BORN: 13 August 1995
Beaumont-sur-Oise,
France

HEIGHT: 1.89 m

POSITION: Defender

PROFESSIONAL CAREER:
Paris Saint-Germain FC,
Qatar SC

DID YOU KNOW?

In October 2016, to compensate for Eliaquim Mangala's injury, Didier Deschamps appealed to a surprised Presnel Kimpembe to join Les Bleus. Having appeared on the international stage with the French U-21 set-up, the 21 year old from Île-de-France had even made one appearance for the Democratic Republic of the Congo, his country of origin, at U-20 level. When the tricolour coach summoned him to Clairefontaine, Kimpembe had only played 13 matches in Ligue 1 with PSG!

Big meaty slaps on the thighs of Paul Pogba and Samuel Umtiti, the images seared into the minds of supporters. In the documentary *Les Bleus 2018, The Russian Epic* by Emmanuel Le Ber and Théo Schuster, the luxury joker Presnel Kimpembe teased two of the tricolour pillars of that success who sit and suffer in silence. Just like Benjamin Mendy's dancing, the reputation of the young Parisian defender was made, that of a playful boy loving life, certainly a joker but with an extraordinary mind.

His first trainers at PSG struggled to recognise the ability of the clumsy teenager who didn't really know what to do with his feet. Today, the player his partners call 'Presko'

exudes a rare serenity for a defender of his age. Nothing frightens him: he remedies any situation with a relaxed and calm air. In the absences of stars such as Thiago Silva or Marquinhos or in the event of the transfer of one of the two Brazilians, Presnel stood strong.

At the age of 24 the left-sided central defender was already a multi-champion of France with PSG, and despite a poor post–World Cup in 2018 he remained a safe bet in Ligue 1. With a constant desire to defend while remaining on his feet, the native of Beaumont-sur-Oise has valuable technical quality on each side. The kid from Éragny, a town in Val-d'Oise where he grew up, had come a long way.

Despite some setbacks Presnel Kimpembe gritted his teeth. 'I have always believed in myself. With the club, it was complicated but I hung on,' the Ile-de-France resident recalled. An adept at pressing, he convinced Laurent Blanc to launch him into the fray, the boss giving a vote of confidence to the elegant defender. Unai Emery also reinforced Presnel's conviction to go into battle relentlessly.

If all was well at the start with Thomas Tuchel, the German coach did not appreciate the opinion of Presnel Kimpembe. Following the Champions League elimination at the hands of Manchester United on away goals, Tuchel questioned the quality of the Parisian group. Kimpembe had actually scored his first professional goal at Old Trafford in the first leg. Kimpembe continued to impress before heading to the Middle East, PSG allowing him to sign for Qatar SC.

FRANCE

Randal

KOLO MUANI

BORN: 5 December 1998
Bondy, France

HEIGHT: 1.88 m

POSITION: Forward

PROFESSIONAL CAREER:
FC Nantes, Boulogne, Eintracht Frankfurt, Paris Saint-Germain FC, Tottenham Hotspur FC (loan)

DID YOU KNOW?

For his first match in the Bundesliga on 5 August 2022, Randal Kolo Muani experienced a disastrous baptism of fire. At Deutsche Bank Park in Frankfurt, the stronghold of European banks, Bayern Munich went to the cash register. Benjamin Pavard was among the goal scorers as Munich triumphed 6–1, Frankfurt's new number 9 finding the net in response on debut. It was of scant consolation, but it was a sign of things to come for the French striker.

On 18 December 2022 in Qatar in Lusail Stadium, which had already borne witness to one of the most epic football contests in history and had the watching crowd breathless, Argentina and France were deadlocked at 3–3 after 120 minutes of end-to-end exhilarating action in the FIFA World Cup final. As the seconds ticked away to the inevitable penalty shoot-out, a long ball from Ibrahima Konaté split the Argentine defence. Suddenly, Randal Kolo Muani found himself free, bearing down one on one with Argentina goalkeeper Emiliano Martínez. The forward had a fraction of a second to decide what to do as the custodian advanced, and his effort from the right of the area was superbly blocked by a player who would be named as the Golden Glove of the tournament.

It was harsh on a player who had made the difference for his team. Introduced in the 41st minute for Ousmane Dembélé, the French were adrift of their opponents, trailing 0–2 to a Leo Messi-inspired display and seemingly down and out, but Kolo Muani became the detonator of the unlikely comeback. It was he who won the penalty after being caught by Nicolás Otamendi, Kylian Mbappé doing the honours from the spot and reigniting hope in Les Bleus camp. However, it was not to be, and after the denouement of his saved chance Argentina won on penalties.

Far from destroying him psychologically, the former Nantes resident decided to use this mishap to bounce back. When he scored the opening goal against Morocco in the semi-finals, a 2–0 success, 'Kolo' found it hard to believe. It had taken an incredible combination of circumstances for him to even participate in the global fest. The career of the striker originally of Congolese culture has always had this taste for permanent miracles.

After developing at different clubs in the Parisian suburbs Randal got his foot in the door of training centres from Stéphanois and Rennes, but in vain. Nantes was the dream outcome but, here again, the future was darkening. Immature, Kolo was late for training most of the time so the Canaries staff sent him to toughen up at US Boulogne in the rough national championship. His return to Nantes was a success, punctuated by the Coupe de France win in 2022. The striker set sail to the Bundesliga the following summer, joining Eintracht Frankfurt. In a sensational debut year he played 53 matches, scoring 24 goals and creating 15 others. This led to a move back to France and the bright lights of the capital, joining PSG before a move on loan to Tottenham Hotspur.

FRANCE

Ibrahima

KONATÉ

BORN: 25 May 1999
Paris, France

HEIGHT: 1.94 m

POSITION: Centre back

PROFESSIONAL CAREER:
Sochaux_Montbéliard, RB Leipzig, Liverpool

On the grounds of Melwood in the suburbs of Liverpool, 'Ibou' rolled his eyes. 'In the early days I looked around me: it was incredible. In the locker room to my right was Virgil van Dijk [and] to my left Thiago Alcântara. They are guys I play with on FIFA!' When he arrived with the Reds in the summer of 2021 Ibrahima Konaté, on top of his game at just 22 years of age, had every reason to be impressed. However, the young Parisian of Malian origin is rarely flustered by his surroundings. It helped that his new coach, German Jürgen Klopp, was already a huge fan. 'I'm really happy that we were able to add Ibrahima to our team,' Klopp said. 'His physical qualities are very impressive: he is fast, very strong and dominant in the air.'

Having begun his career training and playing with Sochaux, starting with the team's reserves the Lion Cubs, Ibou did not arrive at Liverpool in unfamiliar territory: the previous four seasons had been spent in the demanding level of the Bundesliga alongside his compatriot Dayot Upamecano at RB Leipzig. Despite the impressive surroundings of Anfield, Konaté blended into the tradition of the club seamlessly and put himself in the pocket of the public who worship at the cathedral on the banks of the Mersey. When his family joined him, everyone was amazed by the ease of his adaptation. He quickly became a benchmark defender: a function that the Franco-Malian has not always held since, because as a teenager he played attack.

It was Reda Bekhti at Paris FC who took him back a notch, setting him up as a sentinel of the back. Then, looping in with his training in Franche-Comté near the Bonal Stadium, Konaté developed into a centre back of incredible power. With such a background and seeing a player who was certainly still juvenile but already endowed with vast experience, Didier Deschamps could not remain indifferent at national level.

To compensate for the absence of Raphaël Varane, in June 2022 Deschamps called Konaté up for the Nations League and Ibou debuted in Vienna, alongside William Saliba in the middle of the defence, in a 1–1 draw against Austria. Less than six months later came the adventure in Qatar during the FIFA World Cup, in which the Parisian defender appeared five times in seven matches. The kid from La Roquette, in the 11th district of the capital, came close to the Holy Grail against Argentina. He felt that the defeat was just a postponement: the future belongs to him.

DID YOU KNOW?

Son Goku wants to save the world, and the hero of Dragon Ball inspires Ibrahima Konaté. A Manga fan, the French defender does not hide the fact that he sometimes projects himself in the manner of this Japanese comic book hero. 'His mentality inspires me enormously,' Konaté said. 'I don't look at my competitors; I focus on my own person and seek to reach the best possible level.' That's no problem as long as he doesn't fly to Vegeta, the planet where his favourite characters live . . .

Jules

KOUNDÉ

BORN: 12 November 1998
Paris, France

HEIGHT: 1.84 m

POSITION: Defender

PROFESSIONAL CAREER:
Bordeaux, Séville FC,
FC Barcelona

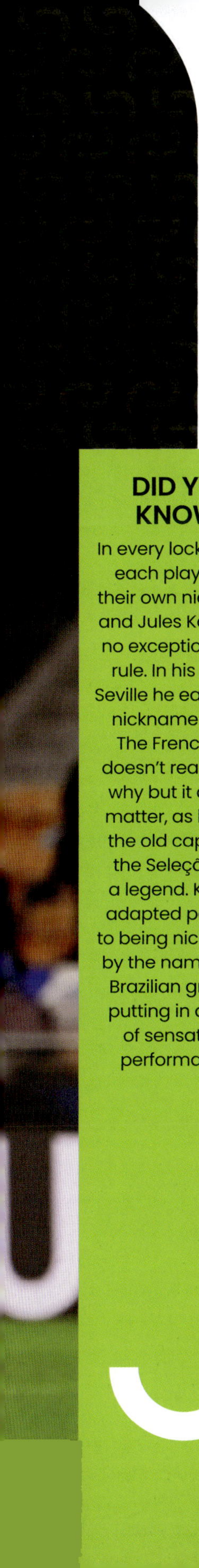

Everywhere and nowhere at the same time. Versatility is sometimes a naughty word, but you won't hear any complaints from Jules Koundé. If he plays centrally in his club team or he's deployed wider out in the colours of his national squad it matters little to this composed defender, who imposes himself on the action wherever he is selected.

Nicknamed the 'quiet strength' by those around him, Koundé was thrown into the deep end of the professional game by Jocelyn Gourvennec one evening in January 2018 in Granville, during a Coupe de France match that was played in nightmare conditions. In the wind and rain, and seeing his team reduced to nine men after two players were sent off, he was one of the few to emerge with any credit. The experience was tough but he validated his place in the team, a single appearance enough to establish his presence as an essential element of the Girondins Bordeaux defence in Ligue 1.

Born in Paris, little Koundé grew up in Gironde in Landiras in the middle of the Graves vineyards. Let go by Sochaux-Montbéliard but spotted via Bordeaux, he went through the stages of progression at his own pace. He was captain of the Bordeaux U-19 team, champions of France in 2017, but was snubbed by French youth teams up to the U-20s. It's a path that is a mirror of the image he portrays: that of a peaceful, discreet but assertive character.

Bordeaux managed to keep him for another season (70 matches, 4 goals in total) but finally let him go to Sevilla FC in the summer of 2019 for a substantial sum for a player of this age: €25 million.

With the French U-21 team Koundé was captain of the team in all eight of the matches he played in before he came knocking on the door of the first team, in contention for the Euro 2020 squad. His assurance and application in training were enough to convince Didier Deschamps that he could play a role in the European championship beyond being simply a top-class addition to a stacked bench.

He made his debut on 2 June 2021 in a friendly against Wales, coming on for left back Benjamin Pavard at half-time, and started the Nations League final win over Spain that same year. It was a meteoric rise, and things accelerated even more following this success as the world's biggest clubs came sniffing around. Eventually, he took the plunge and elected for a shift to Xavi's Barça in 2022.

DID YOU KNOW?

In every locker room each player has their own nickname, and Jules Koundé is no exception to the rule. In his club in Seville he earned the nickname 'Cafu'! The Frenchman doesn't really know why but it doesn't matter, as he says the old captain of the Seleção was a legend. Koundé adapted perfectly to being nicknamed by the name of the Brazilian great by putting in a string of sensational performances.

SWEDEN

Dejan KULUSEVSKI

BORN: 25 April 2000
Stockholm, Sweden

HEIGHT: 1.86 m

POSITION: Attacker

PROFESSIONAL CAREER:
Atalanta BC,
Parme Calcio 1913,
Juventus FC,
Tottenham Hotspur FC

Inevitably, the comparison is made on a systematic and regular basis: originally from the Balkans and Viking by adoption, could Dejan Kulusevski be the new Zlatan? Although Ibrahimović was one of his idols when he grew up in the Vällingby district, on the walls of his bedroom the wallpaper was covered instead by Ronaldinho posters. If there is a sporting comparison to be made on the field, it is obvious that Kulusevski has more of the genius of the Brazilian than of the giant of Malmö. And if 'Ibra' has never tried the international adventure in the Bosnian jersey, Kulusevski got closer to the federation of his origin – Macedonia – at a younger age by agreeing to play five matches in the red jersey of the national U-16 team.

Kulusevski's early years at IF Brommapojkarna confirmed his hopes. He perfected his technique in futsal during the endless Scandinavian winter months. He is a pure box-to-box player with an ability to move from goal to goal. Arsenal came looking, but the director of the academy of Bergamo, Maurizio Costanzi, was the more prompt in allowing Atalanta to steal the prodigy. It took just three years for Dejan Kulusevski to start with the primavera team, being called up in January 2019 under the orders of Gian Piero Gasperini.

The boy brought comparisons to Mo Salah. Like the Egyptian, the promising Swede has the power at any time to make the difference and is lightning over 10 m. 'Shady' loves to play on the right side, before cutting infield to better allow his devastating left foot to do its work. He was loaned to Parma to gain playing time and there his reputation in Italy swelled, in particular thanks to his capacity to create opportunities for others, racking up a number of assists with his decisive passes. Suddenly, Kulusevski was attracting the big names of Serie A, especially after he was awarded a maiden Swedish international cap in November 2019.

It was ultimately Juventus who lured him to their ranks, a further comparison coming when his scurrying style and slender frame recalled that of Eden Hazard. This was not surprising: in his first match he opened the scoring against Sampdoria with a beautifully controlled free kick. At the end of his first year in Turin he was named Best Young Player in Series A. He moved to Tottenham Hotspur in 2022, and after a slow start made his mark, only to be sidelined by injury in in 2025.

DID YOU KNOW?

Having barely landed at Juventus, Dejan Kulusevski showed a lot of nerve. During an interview granted to a Swedish television station the young winger lent himself to a game of express questions, and when the journalist asked him 'Messi or Cristiano Ronaldo?' the ambitious hopeful made a response citing the name of the Argentinian. On the Turin side the fans were the most saddened, and if the Italian press were sensing a scandal they were quickly disappointed. CR7 did not take offence.

GEORGIA

Khvicha
KVARATSKHELIA

BORN: 12 February 2001
Tbilisi, Georgia

HEIGHT: 1.83 m

POSITION: Winger

PROFESSIONAL CAREER:
FC Dinamo Tbilisi, FC Rustavi, FC Lokomotiv Moscow, FC Rubin Kazan, FC Dinamo Batumi, SSC Napoli, Paris Saint-Germain FC

DID YOU KNOW?

The Georgian left winger could have played in Ligue 1, but the many French club directors were panicked by his surname! If Willy Sagnol whispered his name to a few presidents of clubs, no one took the risk of betting on this reinforcement. 'I was even asked to find a Latin nickname for Kvaratskhelia,' revealed the outraged ex-Bayern Munich and French national team defender.

Nicknamed 'Kvaradona' by Neapolitan supporters, the Georgian left winger could have suffered when he arrived at the foot of Vesuvius in July 2022. Imagine the dilemma for the child of Nakifu, just 22 years old and already being compared with the absolute icon Diego Armando Maradona. Khvicha melted into the Gli Azzurri collective with foolproof insurance. The challenge was even more difficult to take on because on this left flank he had to succeed Lorenzo Insigne, who had gone into exile at Toronto FC. The result just 10 months later was that he was one of the main players in the conquest of a third Scudetto for Napoli, which had not had its paws on the Italian Serie A title for 33 years!

What an incredible journey for this slender boy, whose main strength is his quality of striking with both feet and his technical ease, confusing defenders with his wily dribbles and rapid changes of direction. The least we can say is that the path taken by this little genius of the round ball was not linear. After having done his classes in the local championship and with a 2018–19 season at FC Roustavi, Khvicha seemed well on his way to a career in Russia. First loaned to Lokomotiv Moscow, the winger was then transferred to Rubin Kazan. However, in March 2022, after the invasion of Ukraine, he was forced to flee.

Becoming an international and with his reputation reinforced in status by the Frenchman Willy Sagnol, the tightrope walker from Tbilisi refound his feet with a short stint back in his homeland at Dinamo Batumi. To everyone's surprise the Neapolitan leaders put their hands on this nugget, who became the first Georgian to put on the sky-blue jersey. The Neapolitan coach Luciano Spalletti was amazed by his ability to counterattack and constantly vary his offensive options.

His understanding with striker Victor Osimhen was one of the secrets of the success of this Napoli side that revelled in perpetual movement. 'He has one technique worthy of the strongest in the world and this quality of feeling where the goal is to always create the best chances,' insisted Spalletti, talking about a player who always puts him in the best mood. After the surprise effect of his first months, Khvicha continued to confirm his enormous potential and delight his fans. Much sought after, the winger switched to PSG during the January transfer window for a fee of €80 million.

POLAND

Robert
LEWANDOWSKI

BORN: 21 August 1988
Varsovie, Poland

HEIGHT: 1.85 m

POSITION: Striker

PROFESSIONAL CAREER:
Znicz Pruszków,
Lech Poznań,
Borussia Dortmund,
Bayern Munich,
FC Barcelona

DID YOU KNOW?

On 9 March 2019 Bayern Munich pulverised VfL Wolfsburg 6–0. During the game Robert Lewandowski scored twice, and with 197 goals since his Bundesliga debut in 2010 became the all-time top foreign goal scorer, beating the target set by the Peruvian Claudio Pizarro 0f 195 goals. He netted his 200th league goal in a 5–0 win over Dortmund a month later.

He could have been seen in the Tour de France: a big bike lover since he was a kid, Robert Lewandowski put on cycling gear as soon as he had the opportunity to do so in the Bavarian countryside. A sports enthusiast, the Polish striker also indulged in bodybuilding sessions in a furnished room of his villa. Well, as you might understand, Oktoberfest in Germany is not really his thing! A healthy body and a healthy mind: in October 2017 'Lewy' earned a sports management degree. His thesis, 'RL9, path to glory', pleased his fans, who on this occasion were dressed in red and white and had a history of paying homage to their prestigious student.

Lewandowski had an incredible journey to the top flight and its riches, a story that began 10 years earlier as a professional at Znicz Pruszków, in the midst of Mazovia, earning just €500 per month. Some months previously his football career had been almost nipped in the bud when, as a young hopeful at Legia Warszawa, he was unceremoniously fired from the great club of the Polish capital. 'Not tough enough,' they said. Moreover, the teenager had a rather suspect knee, which led the Legia doctors to finding him fragile.

With a mother who was a volleyball player and a dad who practised judo, Lewandowski was blessed with the DNA of a future champion. His career exploded into life at Lech Poznań and then in Germany, where the world began to sit up and take notice of Lewy's prodigious scoring feats.

In the 2010 off-season Borussia Dortmund won the race to snag his signature and so began a decade rich in exploits in the Bundesliga. The Pole is the archetypal centre forward of modern times: strong on both feet, dexterous in the air and with an unexpected versatility.

During his time on the bench of Bayern Munich, the club that took Lewandowski from Dortmund, Pep Guardiola even developed him into an unexpected left winger!

Lewandowski doesn't shirk his defensive responsibilities either, but it's in front of goal that he set record after record with his incredible run of goals at the Bavarian giants. If there is one blight on his career it was arguably his limited impact at major tournaments with Poland. However, he did break his World Cup scoring duck at the 2022 edition in Qatar and hit the ground running amid a blaze of goals at Barcelona, a new chapter in his goal-laden career.

ENGLAND/NIGERIA

Ademola

LOOKMAN

BORN: 20 October 1997, Wandsworth, England

HEIGHT: 1.75 m

POSITION: Winger

PROFESSIONAL CAREER: Charlton Athletic FC, Everton FC, RB Leipzig (loan), RB Leipzig, Fulham (loan), Leicester City FC (loan), Atalanta

Did you know?

Forty-nine years of waiting: you have to go back to 1975 to find evidence of a hat-trick in a European final. Back then, in the colours of winners Borussia Mönchengladbach in the UEFA Cup (now known as the Europa League), Germany's Jupp Heynckes scored three goals against FC Twente in Enschede, Netherlands in a 5–1 win. Lookman has now joined that rarefied company.

It's not often you get to compete in an international final and score a hat-trick, but that's what happened to the intrepid Ademola Lookman in Dublin on 22 May 2024 in the climax of the Europa League. The showdown in Europe's secondary club competition pitted Lookman's Atalanta against German giants Bayer 04 Leverkusen, a team that had not lost a game in any competition up to that point in the season. However, Lookman was to have his night of nights, scoring all three goals in a 3–0 victory. When asked by a reporter how he felt after his memorable feat, the striker simply said: 'This is one of the best days of my life!'

For this football miracle worker the story is a beautiful one. As a teenager his trials with London clubs were unsuccessful. He had no choice but to join Waterloo FC and play in the modest Sunday league until he was aged 16. Ademola grew up south of the Thames in a Nigerian family whose father remained in Lagos. He joined Charlton Athletic Academy, where he completed his training before turning professional in 2015 with the Addicks.

Lookman discovered the tough battles of the championship in the English second tier the following season, and even though the club was relegated he was named best player in the division. In January 2017, before his 20th birthday, his goal was achieved as Premier League Everton signed him. For two years with the Toffees, Ronald Koeman, Sam Allardyce and then Marco Silva gave him his chance: he played in 48 matches.

In July 2019 Lookman embarked on a new adventure in the Bundesliga under the burgeoning stewardship of Julian Nagelsmann; however, the highly rated coach made little use of him. After the COVID-19 and confinement episode, Lookman rediscovered his taste for a return to England, first on loan to Fulham and then to Leicester City.

In August 2022 he headed for Lombardy to discover Serie A in Italy with Atalanta. With a stable squad, Lookman was finally able to highlight his versatile and creative skills as a winger and was always on the move. Blessed with explosive and dynamic movement, he is good with both feet and adept at fast transitions.

After a spell in the England national teams – from U-19s to the juniors, including a World Championship title with the U-20s in Korea in 2017 – the striker of African descent began to question his international options. In the end, in March 2022 he opted to join the Super Eagles of Nigeria at senior level with the firm intention of shining in the land of his ancestors.

BELGIUM

Romelu

LUKAKU

BORN: 13 May 1993
Antwerp, Belgium

HEIGHT: 1.91 m

POSITION: Striker

PROFESSIONAL CAREER:
Anderlecht, Chelsea FC,
West Bromwich Albion FC,
Everton FC,
Manchester United FC,
Inter Milan, AS Roma,
SSC Napoli

DID YOU KNOW?

A true force of nature, Romelu Lukaku experienced very rapid growth. He was already so big and massive as a child that he had to constantly justify his age in the youth categories. His first trainer, Erwin Wosky, recalled it well: 'At nine years old he already had adult shoes. The coaches did not believe that he was that young; he had to carry his passport everywhere with him to prove it. The other children literally started crying when they saw him coming. He was a monster.'

When young, Romelu Lukaku never thought of being a football star. The kid from Antwerp had an old head on young shoulders, and despite being ahead of his peers on the pitch he just wanted to play football and enjoy himself on the field. False modesty, or a lack of ambition? Probably the former, as Lukaku is the top scorer in the history of the Belgian national team, having netted 68 goals in 104 internationals at the culmination of the 2022 FIFA World Cup in Qatar.

As a child he already dreamed of annihilating his opponents. 'I was trying to rip the leather off the ball every time I kicked it. No finesse shooting. I wasn't kidding. I was trying to kill you.'

While not always orthodox in this technique, Lukaku is not just a man mountain and a huge physical specimen ready to bulldoze his way to individual glory. Indeed, he is more of an altruistic centre forward, wedded to the good of the team. It's in his nature.

A difficult childhood in the middle of a penniless family for whom the electricity bills each month proved to be a headache inspired a driving force to achieve. In a confession published on The Players' Tribune website, the ex-Manchester United player described a daily life of poverty. One anecdote from when he was aged six left a telling mark: 'I caught my mother adding water to my bowl of milk,' Lukaku remembered. 'The same as the day before. I realised then that we were broke. Not just poor: broke. That day I knew exactly what I had to do and what I was going to do.'

From there it was a goal-laden story, with bags of goals wherever the left footer took his 1.91 m and 94 kg frame. His first professional contract was with Belgian side Anderlecht, signing for the perennial Belgian champions when he had just turned 16. After winning the Belgian title and scooping the top scorer gong, the striker was on the move to England.

Not really given much of a chance at Chelsea, he exploded at Everton with 87 goals in four seasons, awakening the interest of the big Premier League clubs. A switch to Manchester United yielded 42 goals in 96 appearances before Lukaku headed to Italy and a prolific spell with Internazionale. A tumultuous few years followed for the striker, with a brief return to Chelsea followed by loan spells with Inter Milan and AS Roma, the latter under José Mourinho. A mangled transfer saga was finally drawn to a conclusion when Lukaku signed for Napoli for the 2024–25 campaign.

BRAZIL

MARQUINHOS

BORN: 14 May 1994
São Paulo, Brazil

HEIGHT: 1.83 m

POSITION: Defender

PROFESSIONAL CAREER:
Corinthians SP, AS Roma, Paris Saint-Germain FC

DID YOU KNOW?

At the age of 25 Marquinhos was one of the best defenders in the world, but his fate could have been very different. The younger Marquinhos touched his first footballs as a goalkeeper playing in the small futsal club SACI, and according to his coaches at the time the lad was good in goal. However, one day he moved up the pitch to troubleshoot in defence, and the rest is known.

PSG sometimes looked like the Seleção: a colony of Brazilian internationals frequently seen dancing the samba in the French locker room. Neymar, Thiago Silva, Dani Alves . . . but the best of them all was not necessarily the one grabbing the most headlines. However, this player was the most essential, most efficient one in the long term, rarely injured and always ready to play for the good of the team in a position that might not necessarily be his best. This is Marquinhos.

Marquinhos, whose real name is Marcos Aoás Corrêa, is a blessing for a coach: he is a discreet footballer with indisputable quality and incredible value. This is why every summer the biggest clubs – Juventus and FC Barcelona being just two to have shown interest – knock on the door of PSG to make an offer, which the Parisian club does not even consider. Marquinhos is not for sale at any price!

Equipped with an impressive maturity from an early age, Marquinhos is a complete central defender. Fast and efficient in his interceptions, the Brazilian has a rare sense of placement and an amazing vision of the game from his position as central defender. Looking back, in his life as a footballer everything happened very quickly. A professional at the age of 17 in the jersey of Corinthians of São Paulo, Marquinhos quickly went to Europe, to Roma, where he won the hearts of the supporters in double time. He even earned a first call-up for the Brazilian national team while he was still young enough to sport traces of acne on his face.

The big European clubs were courting him, and it was the Qatar-backed Paris Saint-Germain that raided the bank to secure his services for a cool €35 million. At that price some were saying only time would tell whether it was a good deal, and six years after his arrival in the French capital it can be ascertained that he was an absolute gift. Given the prices that defenders are beginning to attract, the fee is a steal.

Marquinhos soon became a regular member of the squad and an almost omnipresent figure in the national selection, from which he won the Olympic gold medal in Rio. He benefited from the presence of defensive colleague Miranda, who had been installed in the Seleção after the fiasco of the 2014 World Cup. With his impeccable French, Marquinhos is a potential captain near the Porte d'Auteuil, and while he may not be the flashiest Brazilian seen at the Parc des Princes he is a vital part of a star-studded line-up.

ARGENTINA

Emiliano
MARTÍNEZ

BORN: 2 September 1992, Mar Del Plata, Argentina

HEIGHT: 1.95 m

POSITION: Goalkeeper

PROFESSIONAL CAREER: Arsenal FC, Oxford United (loan), Sheffield Wednesday FC (loan), Rotherham United FC (loan), Wolverhampton Wanderers (loan), Getafe CF (loan), Reading FC (loan), Aston Villa FC

DID YOU KNOW?

Because of his resemblance to a cartoon character popular with children in Argentina, Emiliano was nicknamed 'Dibu' by former Independiente goalkeeper Miguel Ángel Santoro. The new name stuck and particularly in the dressing room, where the Argentinian goalkeeper is particularly appreciated for his team spirit and closeness to his teammates.

First things first: yes, Emiliano Dibu Martínez is a born provocateur. Since 18 December 2022 and that penalty shoot-out in the final of the World Cup in Qatar, the Argentinian goalkeeper has been in the crosshairs of French fans. Yes, his obscene gestures have crossed the line. Yes, his appearance in Lille (his first in France) in April 2024 during the Europa Conference League quarter final against LOSC reinforced his ugly duckling image.

Once the annoying behaviour page is out of the way, though, there is no mistaking that Emiliano is an exemplary goalkeeper. His physical presence in the box, anticipation, aerial ability and reflexes on the line are a delight. Trained at Independiente, he distinguished himself at an early age with the Diablos Rojos in Avellaneda.

Before he turned 18 Emiliano opted for a transfer to Arsenal. He played with the Gunners' reserves and accepted repeated loans to gain playing time in the English lower tiers. Ten years later, taking advantage of Bernd Leno's injury, the Argentinian moved into the Arsenal goal, and after the COVID-19 pandemic took part in the summer's FA Cup final against Chelsea. Thanks to a brace from Pierre-Emerick Aubameyang in the 2–1 victory, the Gunners won the trophy.

Martínez was keen to regain his number 1 position in the Arsenal goal, but Mikel Arteta gave the starting shirt back to Bernd Leno. With only 39 games in eight seasons with the Gunners, Dibu decided to move, and for around €20 million he was transferred to Aston Villa. In view of his performances, Lionel Scaloni retained him for the Copa América 2021 in Brazil.

Martínez stood out in the semi-finals against Colombia, saving three penalties in the shoot-out before Argentina clinched their 15th continental title in their history, surprising the Seleção, Brazil 1–0 in the final. Martinez went on to become an essential cornerstone of the Argentine squad with his epic performances in Qatar, becoming a world champion in the most beautiful of ways and enjoyed by most: except for Les Bleus fans!

ARGENTINA

Lautaro
MARTÍNEZ

BORN: 22 August 1997
Bahía Blanca, Argentina

HEIGHT: 1.74 m

POSITION: Striker

PROFESSIONAL CAREER:
Racing Club de Avellaneda,
FC Inter Milan

DID YOU KNOW?

At the age of 18 Lautaro Martínez, with a tempered steel character, refused an offer from the prestigious Real Madrid club because he wanted to succeed first in the colours of Racing Club, notably in the Copa Libertadores, before leaving for Europe. This was an extremely rare fact that was revealed by the president of the Argentina team, Victor Blanco, in person, in the daily newspaper *Mundo Deportivo*.

In the near future Lautaro Martínez could well be mentioned in the same breath as some of the greatest Argentinean goal scorers such as Mario Kempes and Carlos Tevez. Why? Because 'El Toro' is not only an incredible competitor who plays with physicality and aggressiveness but is also an amazing goal hunter. With these qualities he recalls a certain Gabriel Batistuta. Others find his a hybrid style between that of Gonzalo Higuaín and Sergio Agüero.

When during the Copa América 2019 no less than Lionel Messi dubbed this capable striker 'outstanding' thanks to his versatility to play in any system – as a pure centre forward, as part of a pair or even in support of the attacker – we are surely looking at a future superstar.

In December 2018 he entered the hearts of the tifosi of Internazionale in a clash against Napoli, scoring the only goal during additional time: an ideal scenario to ingratiate yourself with your supporters! Five months earlier for the sum of €23 million, Lautaro arrived in the capital of the Lombard region on the advice of Wanda Nara, wife of Mauro Icardi and incidentally a football agent. Lautaro arrived with a good reputation that had been fostered on the other side of the Atlantic.

At Racing Club, one of the many clubs in Buenos Aires, he shone like the light of a thousand fires in the jersey of the Academia. However, not everything was rosy in Argentina, because as a teenager Martínez had been released by Boca Juniors. The bitterness was huge, but he is stubborn. His father Mario, a former player himself, pushed young Lautaro on a daily basis. Mario had never been able to make the breakthrough but he believed in the destiny of his offspring.

Martínez was surprisingly good with his head for someone of modest size, and at Racing Club he even began as a defender. He soon moved further forward and, after 22 goals in 48 matches, alerted the presence of the European giants. Barça tried to recruit the little bull in 2018, but it was Inter who won the race for his signature.

Having made his Argentina debut in March 2018, Martínez netted the winning penalty in the 2022 FIFA World Cup quarter final shoot-out against the Netherlands, sending La Albiceleste into the semi-finals. From there, a World Cup winner with Argentina, he literally had the world at his feet.

FRANCE

Kylian

MBAPPÉ

BORN: 20 December 1998
Paris, France

HEIGHT: 1.78 m

POSITION: Forward

PROFESSIONAL CAREER:
AS Monaco,
Paris Saint-Germain FC,
Real Madrid

DID YOU KNOW?

In the summer of 2011 Kylian Mbappé could have become Norman. On the wish list of Caen, the 13-year-old kid was already attracting covetous glances and the team from the Malherbe stadium was in the running. However, as they were in financial strife at the time the Calvados club tightened its belt and decided not to pay the €60,000 needed to recruit the AS Bondy prodigy; the president of Caen at the time, Jean-François Fortin, preferred to save jobs. Farewell, Kylian, and the young Parisian ended up at the Clairefontaine academy instead.

Born on 30 June 2018 even if, officially, Kylian Mbappé first saw the light of day on 20 December 1998. From a footballing point of view the planet discovered a little wonder on a warm Russian summer day in the Round of 16 at the World Cup. In Kazan Mbappé, a precocious attacker, disintegrated the Argentine defence with a dazzling display. In the 11th minute the boy from Bondy, the son of Fayza and Wilfrid, launched a dazzling counter.

Timed at 37 km/hour, 'Razmoket' ate up the ground before being illegally stopped by Marcos Rojo. The penalty was converted by Antoine Griezmann, which marked the beginning of a tricolour festival. The conclusion was a memorable success at 4–3 that was signed by a double from a kid just 19 years old.

Of course, Kylian Mbappé is no longer an unknown. From his debut with AS Monaco in the Champions League, the cream of European football – Manchester City, Borussia Dortmund, Juventus and the rest – found out about the audacity of the new pearl of French football. Besides his supersonic speed, Mbappé impressed with his maturity on the pitch. With an innate sense of realism and ice cold in front of goal, he tortured opposing goalkeepers.

It wasn't just on the pitch that he was impressive. The disconcerting young man showed remarkable calmness, his comments lucid and at ease in front of the microphone. He presented an intelligent persona, and Mbappé mania swept the globe. A world champion in 2018, scoring in the final win over Croatia and congratulated by King Pelé in person, Mbappé broke all youth records, and not just with his countless goals.

A record transfer to PSG in 2017 brought even more goals and accolades, but the pinnacle on a personal level was about to come. Qatar, 2022: a second FIFA World Cup final, and Mbappé became only the second man ever to net a hat-trick in a global showdown, following England's Geoff Hurst in 1966. His treble helped the game end 3–3, but it was to be Messi's coronation.

The heir apparent to the Argentine phenomenon, he already boasts 12 World Cup finals goals and four in the biggest game on the planet, the final itself. After flirting with Mbappé across several seasons Real Madrid finally landed their latest Galactico on a free transfer, but with mammoth wages, in the summer of 2024. His ascendency to legendary status would surely be complete with a UEFA Champions League crown.

FRANCE

Ferland

MENDY

BORN: 8 June 1995
Meulan-en-Yvelines,
France

HEIGHT: 1.80 m

POSITION: Defender

PROFESSIONAL CAREER:
Le Havre AC,
Olympique Lyonnais,
Real Madrid CF

In the Mendy football family there are Bernard, Benjamin, Édouard, Étienne and all the others who walked the grass and graced the stadiums of Ligue 1, but none of them put down their boots at Real Madrid. Until, that is, Ferland Mendy. Having established himself in the crisp white shirt of the Spanish giants, Ferland can arguably state that he has had the most successful career of them all. His back story is quite a beautiful one.

A move from Le Havre to the mythical club trained by Zinedine Zidane via Lyon in less than two seasons. Has anyone done it better? In record time, Ferland has progressed from Ligue 2, Ligue 1, Olympique Lyonnais and the French national team and is now in the most revered dressing room in the world: a very real dream that has come true. However, if his story was a film it would not be one of a spoiled child.

A chaotic journey sprinkled with discipline problems: Mendy had to work for his success. Passing through the youth formation of Paris Saint-Germain between 2005 and 2012, his career appeared in jeopardy when at the age of 15 he found himself in a wheelchair. Arthritis of the hip, contracted at just 14, saw him leave PSG and his future football career was in doubt.

'For three months I was in the Necker hospital, in plaster,' Ferland recalled. 'The doctors told me that football was over for me; they even spoke to me of amputation.' Fortunately for Ferland and football lovers the world over, he recovered and continued to impress. As a player he hustled and as a man he is humble, well spoken and a great communicator.

The generation he is from is golden: Presnel Kimpembe, Kingsley Coman, Adrien Rabiot, Moussa Dembélé and Ferland Mendy all on the same card. His personality stood out early, as he is never short of jokes and pranks on his mates – behaviour that can perhaps be explained by the disappearance of the father figure. His dad's death was a tipping point that Ferland never speaks about and still today it's impossible to break through the armour. He locks this part of his life well away.

The Norman air of Le Havre gave him his first break, with three seasons and around 50 matches in Ligue 2. He was named as the best left back of the championship. These performances kindled interest elsewhere, and Lyon came calling in 2017. Not seen as a potential starter when joining, he soon confirmed himself as the best left back at the club and before long was living the dream at Real.

DID YOU KNOW?

Before being called by Didier Deschamps to the French team, the Real Madrid defender Ferland Mendy had never been selected with the French youth teams. His serious hip injury when he was in pre-training at Paris Saint-Germain almost forced him to quit football. He discovered the Château de Clairefontaine only when he was selected for the senior national team in 2018.

ARGENTINA

Lionel

MESSI

BORN: 24 June 1987
Rosario, Argentina

HEIGHT: 1.70 m

POSITION: Forward

PROFESSIONAL CAREER:
FC Barcelona,
Paris Saint-Germain FC,
Inter Miami CF

A glorious day in Qatar cemented a legacy. Argentina fulfilled the dream of a player who has graced the stadiums of the world with his sheer brilliance, hoisting the golden trophy that confirmed La Albiceleste as champions of the world. In the eyes of many Lionel Messi was the greatest of all time. The win over France, a penalty shoot-out success after a 3–3 draw in which Messi had struck twice, finally put paid to the suggestions that the diminutive superstar was unable to impose himself in his national team's colours.

The critics had a point up to then. After Argentina had been ousted from the 2018 tournament in Russia by the same French selection, losing by the odd goal in a seven-goal thriller, Messi announced his international retirement. Fortunately for football lovers around the globe, after a few months of abstinence the prodigy returned in March 2019. His comeback match ended in a 1–3 loss to Venezuela in Madrid, but it would of course get better!

The World Cup glory added to the Copa América triumph of 2021, Argentina defeating Brazil 1–0 in the final in their great rival's own backyard. It was Messi's first international success at the fifth attempt and it was followed by a triumph in the Finalissima, a 3–0 defeat of European champions Italy at Wembley Stadium. Messi played a major part with a brace of assists.

Despite serious concerns about his growth in his adolescence, the young Argentinian was well nurtured by FC Barcelona at their iconic La Masia, the renowned training centre. Catalan educators loved the young boy who had landed in their midst like a gift from the South American gods. The kid from Rosario in northern Argentina was already the darling of his local club of Newell's Old Boys. The Catalan doctors imposed a heavy treatment based on hormone injections so the undersized Messi would not be handicapped by his stature.

At just 17 years of age and having forged an athletic body, Leo Messi discovered La Liga with the great Barça, making a debut in 2004 that marked the beginning of a story embroidered in golden letters. The immortal Argentinean exploded onto the scene with the Blaugrana and began a trophy haul that saw him claim seven Ballon d'Or awards. His time at Camp Nou ended in a tearful media conference in 2021 as he moved to PSG where, it's fair to say, his star was undimmed despite not always winning over the supporters. He latterly switched to MLS in the USA and signed for Inter Miami to write a whole new chapter.

DID YOU KNOW?

A quintuplet and two assists in a 16–0 victory meant Messi was on fire in the shirt of Barcelona as he racked up these impressive numbers. However, it was not Lionel but his son Thiago, who at just six years of age was following in the footsteps of his father. With his youth team at La Masia, Messi Junior shone on the pitch but also had a critical eye. 'He likes to look at me, ask me questions and, when things are bad, he gives me grades,' dad Leo laughed.

GERMANY

Jamal

MUSIALA

BORN: 26 February 2003, Stuttgart, Germany

HEIGHT: 1.84 m

POSITION: Attacking midfielder, forward

PROFESSIONAL CAREER: Bayern Munich II, Bayern Munich

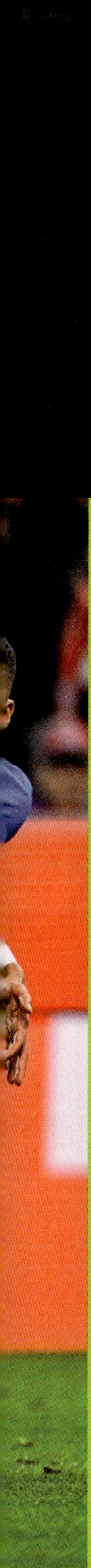

When Jamal Musiala came on against SC Freiburg in June 2020 in a 3–1 victory, not only did he become the youngest player in Bayern Munich history to take part in a Bundesliga match but the young German prodigy also replaced club legend Thomas Müller. There are few more impressive ways to make a debut.

In February 2021 when he replaced Thomas Müller on the pitch of the Olimpico Stadium in Rome, he replicated Robert Lewandowski and Leroy Sané by scoring his first UEFA Champions League goal against SS Lazio in a match in which Bayern strolled to a 4–1 success. In June that year the Stuttgart native became the youngest player to represent the German national team in a major tournament, launched into action by Joachim Löw against Hungary. The game was played in his usual backyard, Munich's Allianz Arena, and ended in a 2–2 stalemate.

Jamal Musiala's dribbling skills are reminiscent of Brazilian great Ronaldinho. Thanks to his enthusiasm he knows how to get out of pressure situations perfectly, and he is also elusive in his game-making initiatives, which create openings for many others.

Jamal grew up with his parents in Hesse, Germany, playing junior football with TSV Lehnerz. When he was aged seven the family moved to Southampton in the United Kingdom. Already attracted to the game that was the best lever for integration into a new country, the kid became a Saint when he signed in the U-8 category with Southampton.

Musiala was already on the radar of Chelsea, who were doing everything in their power to bring him to London. They succeeded in their goal, and for eight years the youngster's studs trod the pitches of Cobham, the Blues' training centre.

In 2019 he decided on a return to Germany. Bayern were delighted to sign him, and it wasn't long before Musiala was making his mark with the Roten reserve team. A close friend of Jude Bellingham, magic Musiala left an impression on Bayern fans in May 2023. On the 34th and final day of the Bundesliga against FC Cologne, he scored a decisive late goal to clinch the league title – the 33rd in their history – for the Bavarian giants.

The following season was more mixed with a string of injuries and, in sporting terms, the loss of the German title and failure in the UEFA Champions League. Despite these setbacks 'Bambi' once again became a hunter, ready to face any challenge without ever shirking his responsibilities.

DID YOU KNOW?

Jamal Musiala was capped by England! In November 2020 he took his first international steps on debut for the Three Lions juniors against Andorra in a 3–1 win in Wolverhampton. The DFB reacted swiftly, with Oliver Bierhoff, the former head of the German FA, immediately paying him a visit and presenting him with a jersey signed by NBA star Klay Thompson. This gesture tipped the scales in Musiala's favour.

GERMANY

Manuel

NEUER

BORN: 27 March 1986
Gelsenkirchen, Germany

HEIGHT: 1.93 m

POSITION: Goalkeeper

PROFESSIONAL CAREER:
FC Schalke 04,
Bayern Munich

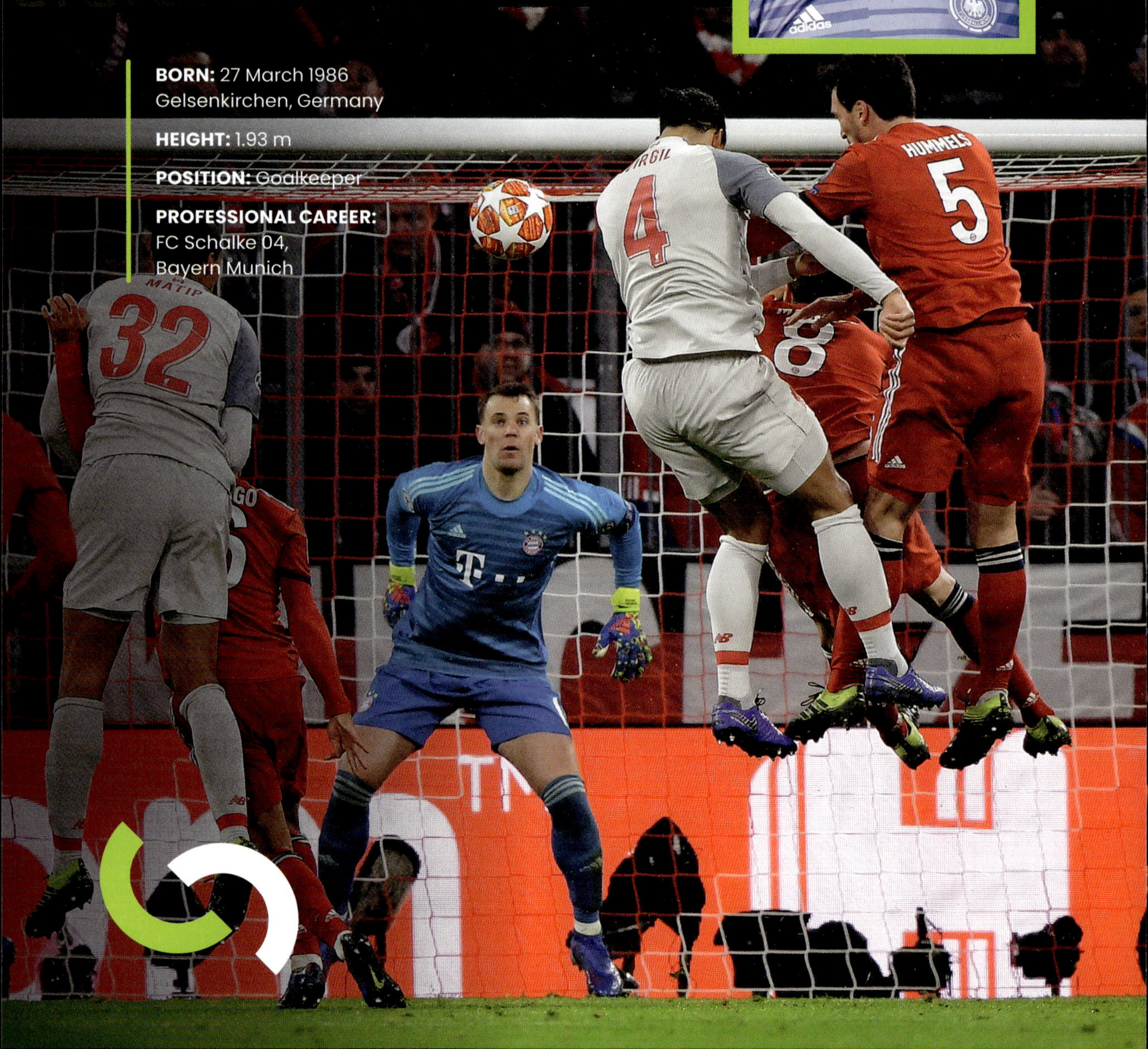

The kid felt his wings growing. In the middle of a match it wasn't rare for young Manuel Neuer to abandon his own penalty area and go on the attack. His father Peter confirmed it, remembering of his 10-year-old son: 'Manuel loved his position as goalkeeper, but he wanted so much to participate in the game!'

Despite a certain technical ease, at the time the teenager was in the crosshairs of his trainers. In the youth categories at Schalke 04 and despite excellent performances and attendance at training, the judgement was that he was too frail. It took the intervention of Lothar Matuschak, one of the best coaches across the Rhine, and the Schalke 04 management to save young Neuer's place at the training centre. Matuschak was convinced that young Manuel was exceptional and had a football brain to go along with the physical presence.

The following year after a late growth spurt, the budding goalkeeper shot up a huge 20 cm and his body thickened, and he now measures 1.93 m and 92 kg. 'He became imposing in his goal,' one of his coaches, Bodo Menze, remembered, 'but Manuel also had very fluid, coordinated movements, like those of a ballet dancer.' His technical audacity also offered solutions to his team.

He was considered to be a first attacker thanks to his eye and his precision passing with his feet and know-how to initiate actions. As a youth 'BeckenNeuer' turned pro at Schalke, and within a few months he was installed in place of incumbent goalkeeper Frank Rost. In the spring of 2011 a choice needed to be made: the proposal of a contract from Bayern Munich had landed on the table of the Neuer family. It provided strength of roots and love of the jersey against ambition and the promise of a shot at all the main prizes.

Neuer, the former ultra of the Nordkurve of the Veltins-Arena, finally gave in to the Bavarian siren call. Glory and titles were within reach, not just with the Roten but also in the jersey of former world champion Germany in Brazil. Neuer manned the goal as the Germans won the tournament with a 1–0 win over Argentina in the final in Rio. It was a great comeback for the keeper, who had been plagued with injuries that kept him off the field for several months, including an operation on his foot.

DID YOU KNOW?

Young Afghan, Iraqi or Syrian refugees sometimes come across their idol. In 2014 Manuel Neuer created the Manuel Neuer Kids Foundation in the Buer district in Gelsenkirchen, a sociocultural structure that accommodates 100 children from troubled families. Despite his privileged status, the goalkeeper of the Nationalmannschaft has not forgotten his proletarian origins in a Ruhr in full deindustrialisation, the very place where he grew up.

BRAZIL

NEYMAR

BORN: 5 February 1992
Mogi das Cruzes, Brazil

HEIGHT: 1.75 m

POSITION: Forward

PROFESSIONAL CAREER:
Santos FC, FC Barcelona, Paris Saint-Germain FC, Al Hilal SFC, Santos FC

There is a Brazilian saying that 'Lightning never strikes twice in the same place, but in Santos she fell three times: for Pelé, for Robinho and for Neymar.' Very soon, all of Brazil had heard about this new genius of national football. Neymar asserted himself at the age of 17 as the new king of Brazilian football.

With the historic club of Pelé he collected titles in spades, including in 2011 a Copa Libertadores, but unlike King Pelé the Neymar clan did not resist the call of the big European clubs. Barça won the race for him, with an official bid of €57 million. In his first clásico against Real Madrid the new number 11 opened the scoring for a 2–1 victory for Barça.

Neymar stacked up the trophies in Catalonia, a sign of his talent being the *remontada* (comeback) that was fatal to PSG in the Champions League. Paris then decided to break the bank for the talented Brazilian, capturing him for an eye-watering €222 million. Neymar, in the shadow of Lionel Messi at Barcelona, arrived at Paris Saint-Germain as a rock star. Greeted at the Parc des Princes like the Messiah, he graced Ligue 1 with his class and even took over the penalty duties from Uruguayan goal machine Edinson Cavani.

Neymar bagged a domestic treble in his first season at the club, scoring 28 times in 30 matches, the first clutch of a swathe of prizes and goals at the Parisian giants. As much as the owners were happy with their continuous sweeping of the board locally, success in Europe was their driving ambition. With Neymar teaming up with young sensation Kylian Mbappé, hope sprung eternal.

On the international stage Neymar made his debut in 2010 in a fixture against the United States in New Jersey, but it was the World Cup in 2014 that was supposed to be his coronation. An untimely back injury, suffered in the quarter-final match against Colombia when he was caught by a knee from Juan Camilo Zúñiga, kept him out of the semi-final and he was forced to watch on as his team was humiliated in front of their adoring public by Germany 7–1.

His time at PSG often flattered to deceive, and he moved to Al Hilal in August 2023. The transfer fee was reported to be worth €90 million, making him the most expensive purchase in the Saudi Pro League, but he only made a handful of appearances in a disappointing spell before moving home to Brazil with first club Santos in January 2025.

DID YOU KNOW?

As an ultrasound was too expensive for the Neymar family, his parents didn't know the sex of their son until the day of his birth. His mum's favourite name was Mateus, but the family was hesitant. For a week Baby Neymar remained without a first name, until the day his dad, Neymar Senior, decided to declare his birth. With his wife they opted for Mateus, but on the way his father changed his mind and called him Neymar Junior. Thus, Neymar was born!

FRANCE

Christopher
NKUNKU

BORN: 14 November 1997
Lagny-sur-Marne, France

HEIGHT: 1.75 m

POSITION: Attacker

PROFESSIONAL CAREER:
Paris Saint-Germain FC,
RB Leipzig, Chelsea FC

The common point between Nicolas Anelka, Kingsley Coman, Moussa Diaby and Christopher Nkunku? They all play in an offensive position but are able to play elsewhere if required, and at different times they all went to seek their happiness far from their training club. Does PSG have a problem with its young people? Seemingly unable to keep their best youth or to offer them serious playing time at the club, the wisp of RB Leipzig is no exception.

After playing just 55 matches in five seasons Nkunku took his talents to the Bundesliga, where he became a star of the German championship, a French international and someone who was linked with a rumoured return to his former stomping ground. Everyone who has ever met Nkunku is unanimous: he feels football and does not shy away from the task at hand.

It is true that the small lad from Lagny-sur-Marne was not an obvious addition to the heavyweight court of European attackers. From his early days as a youngster he was smaller than his friends and certainly frailer. Thus he saw himself obliged by nature to become a different player, limiting his touches of the ball to the strict minimum and condemned to avoid the physical duels but able to read the game faster than other players on the field. He then naturally developed his own qualities of speed, stamina, technical qualities and a fierce shot.

Nkunku arrived at PSG in 2010 and was built up by also playing at the INF Clairefontaine academy before logically integrating into the youth section of the Parisian club. In his early stages he nevertheless had to be protected by his trainers for fear of seeing him break in two, such was his slight physique.

Young and talented, it appeared as though Nkunku had a bright future ahead of him in Paris, but the Parisian competition crushed everything in its passage. After beefing up his game and in Germany and on the European scene, Nkunku was named best player of the Bundesliga in the spring of 2022. It was deserved recognition in front of the stars of Bayern Munich and one more argument towards him becoming essential within the band in France's blue jersey under Didier Deschamps.

Nkunku was called up to the senior French squad for the first time for friendly matches against Ivory Coast and South Africa in March 2022, and he secured a mega-money move to Chelsea in the English Premier League in time for the start of the 2023–24 season.

DID YOU KNOW?

Unlike the younger generation, who are fans of Lionel Messi and Cristiano Ronaldo, Christopher Nkunku is rather admiring of another style. For a long time the Brazilian Willian was his favourite player. The profile of the former international was closer to his: a modest size, lively, technical and an outstanding passer. During the summer of 2015, invited by Laurent Blanc to participate in the preparation of the Parisian club in the United States, the kid fulfilled his dream: to meet his idol.

NORWAY

Martin
ØDEGAARD

BORN: 17 December 1998, Drammen, Norway

HEIGHT: 1.78 m

POSITION: Midfielder

PROFESSIONAL CAREER: Strømsgodset, Real Madrid Castilla, Real Madrid, SC Heerenveen (loan), Vitesse Arnhem (loan), Real Sociedad (loan), Arsenal FC (loan), Arsenal FC

In May 2015, during a match against Getafe, Carlo Ancelotti asked a 16 year old to replace Cristiano Ronaldo. Martin Ødegaard took his first steps in La Liga, but everything was moving a little too fast for the young Norwegian. Completely uprooted from home and in the middle of a crowded squad while just out of his teens, he was groping his way through.

A few months earlier he had arrived at La Castilla to join the Merengues' reserve team, then managed by Zinedine Zidane. It wasn't easy for Martin to find his place in a dressing room where there were several champions per square metre and so he dragged his feet. Six months later he accepted a loan to SC Heerenveen in the Netherlands. The Scandinavian spent three seasons in the Dutch league, primarily with the Super-Frisons and then with Vitesse Arnhem. It was a revelation: far from the hustle and bustle of Spain, the variety and technical ease the Norwegian genius possessed shone through and he finally broke free.

It all began at an exceedingly early age for the child from Drammen. When aged 15 years and 253 days he became the youngest player ever to pull on the jersey for the Norwegian national team in a friendly match in Stavanger against the United Arab Emirates, with the game ending at 0–0.

After spending most of his youth playing football Ødegaard joined Strømsgodset, and in January 2014 made his debut in the professional squad. After exploits spanning three years in the Netherlands the wind shifted: Zidane wanted Martin back at Real. In November 2020 he started in Milan for a prestigious 2–0 victory over Inter, but the Norwegian remained in the shadows as the weeks went by.

In January 2021 Ødegaard closed the door on the Casa Blanca, where he had only played 14 times, and accepted an offer from Arsenal. On his first outing he was given a start by Mikel Arteta, in support of Pierre-Emerick Aubameyang. By this time he had grown up, and he flourished in a 4–3–3 formation where he could take charge of the game. Six months later his loan became a permanent transfer, and this boyhood Liverpool fan signed for the Gunners.

With its three youthful phenomena of Alexander Sørloth, Erling Haaland and Martin Ødegaard, the Norwegian national team is dreaming of reintegrating into the cream of the international crop and aiming to qualify for the 2026 FIFA World Cup in America.

DID YOU KNOW?

At just six years of age little Martin was struggling to indulge his passion for football: in a country where winter lasts nine months, it was not easy to find a decent pitch worth its name. With the help of club members, his parents invested more than €4,000 to cover a gravel pitch with gleaming artificial turf. The child from Drammen was then able to refine his style and develop his technical game.

FRANCE

Michael

OLISE

BORN: 12 December 2001, Hammersmith, England

HEIGHT: 1.84 m

POSITION: Attacking midfielder, winger

PROFESSIONAL CAREER: Reading FC, Crystal Palace FC, Bayern Munich

Michael Olise is primarily a special talent of rich heritage. Of Nigerian, Algerian and French descent, born in the London borough of Hammersmith and trained at Chelsea and then at Reading, he grew up between several different cultures and styles and combines a little bit of everything. There's African technique, French flair and English rigour. Olise mixes these together and makes this a rare recipe.

At Reading, in the unforgiving English championship, he began to alert the big club to his abilities with his mesmerising short dribbles, millimetre-perfect free kicks and laser vision. Crystal Palace jumped the queue and snagged Olise for just €9 million, one of the deals of the decade. On the right flank Olise plays at his own pace, never in a hurry, as though he can see the game 10 seconds ahead of everyone else. His touches are clean and precise, and always full of meaning.

For Palace against Manchester United he nailed a pitch-perfect free kick in the 91st minute to earn his team a 1–1 draw but he neglected to celebrate a stunning goal, simply lowering his head and getting on with the job. When asked why he responded with a whispered, eloquent tone: 'I was just doing my job.' This was concisely Olise, as he speaks little and answers interviews half-heartedly. His teammates say he is mysterious; however, on the pitch he can change a match in one action. 'Michael, he's a quiet killer,' his former manager at Crystal Palace Patrick Vieira said. 'He plays like he's ahead of everyone else.'

Olise reads the game like a leader even when he's on the wing. He attracts fouls, fixes defences and releases the ball at the right time. He might not run everywhere, but he always seems to be where he needs to be.

At the international level everyone wanted him. France, England, Nigeria and Algeria courted his services, but Olise was in no rush to decide. At the youth level he chose to play for les bleuets in the French junior section, but he didn't close the doors on the other nations. For Olise there was no thunderous declaration, no logo kissed; it was just for the love of the game. In Paris at the 2024 Olympics under the direction of Thierry Henry he was part of the squad that claimed silver, leading to a natural promotion to the senior squad.

Voted rookie of the year in his first season in the Bundesliga, Bayern Munich are happy to have a new kaiser in their ranks.

DID YOU KNOW?

In a match with Crystal Palace against Southampton in 2023, Olise had an extraordinary match. Scoring three goals and adding an assist, he put on an absolute masterclass. After the match a journalist asked him: 'Michael, you just scored your first hat-trick in the Premier League. How do you feel?' Olise frowned and replied simply: 'I scored three goals: are you serious? I was focused on winning.' Incredibly, this was not a joke. Olise was sincere and hadn't even realised he had just scored a hat-trick!.

SPAIN

Dani
OLMO

BORN: 7 May 1998, Terrassa, Spain

HEIGHT: 1.82 m

POSITION: Winger, forward

PROFESSIONAL CAREER:
GNK Dinamo Zagreb, GNK Dinamo Zagreb II,
RB Leipzig,
FC Barcelona

Trained at La Masia, Barça's talent nursery, at the top of the class and a player with great character, Dani Olmo refused the comfort of Barcelona's training facilities and at just 16 years of age chose Croatia. The midfielder signed a deal with Dinamo Zagreb, his reasoning being that he wanted to play. 'I needed minutes, not promises,' Olmo revealed. 'There I was trusted right away.'

He left the spotlight to forge himself away from the hustle and bustle of La Liga, and it paid off. In Zagreb he quickly became the boss: number 10, a technical leader and a decisive player. He won titles, discovered the Champions League and was twice voted best player of the season. It was soon evident that the Croatian League was becoming much too small for him.

Olmo's next direction was Leipzig and the German Bundesliga, where Europe discovered his true skills: a player who thinks faster than the others, and a player who might not be the fastest but was surely one of the smartest. He didn't fit the typical profile of a German player, not playing at 100 kilometres an hour and not betting everything on physical power. Instead, Olmo prefers to scan the action, being the player to provide the decisive pass that breaks defensive lines and, when deciding to shoot, being precise and clinical. 'I don't want to shine for me. I want the team to move forward,' was his early mantra.

With Spain he became a man for the big events, exploding at Euro 2021, winning the Nations League and offering a reprisal of that performance in Germany at Euro 2024. He finished in the list of leading goal scorers at the tournament, where each of his goals was decisive as Spain defeated England 2–1 in the final, a result that once again crowned La Roja as champions of Europe. As a newly crowned king of the continent, Olmo's value was skyrocketing. His new home? His old home, a move back to square one.

Olmo returned to FC Barcelona and a chance to finally express himself in Catalonia, but fate can be fickle. Due to financial problems at Camp Nou the Olmo affair became a bad soap opera, with the Spanish Federation initially blocking the transfer and putting him technically in the ranks of the unemployed and free to move where he wished. However, there was a twist in the tale and the Spanish sports courts finally relented, allowing Olmo to achieve his dream and end the season with the double of championship and cup.

DID YOU KNOW?

Extremely popular in Croatia after a successful stint with Dinamo Zagreb – five championships, three cups and one super cup – Dani Olmo admitted he had been offered Croatian citizenship several times in order to play in the 2018 World Cup in Russia with the team that plays in the famous checked shirts. He refused, and was finally called up by the Roja on 8 November 2019. Coming on in place of Álvaro Morata for his first cap on 15 November, he scored immediately in a 7–0 win over Malta in the Euro 2020 qualifying.

NIGERIA

Victor
OSIMHEN

BORN: 29 December 1998
Lagos, Nigeria

HEIGHT: 1.85 m

POSITION: Striker

PROFESSIONAL CAREER:
VfL Wolfsburg,
Royal Charleroi SC,
Lille OSC,
SSC Napoli, Galatasaray SK

DID YOU KNOW?

During the visit of FC Nantes to Pierre-Mauroy on 11 August 2019, Victor Osimhen was preparing to strike hard in his first match in the LOSC jersey. The Nigerian striker has not forgotten a funny episode from before the match: 'When leaving the bus, José Fonte told me: "If you score two goals, I'll take you to a restaurant." I replied: "Okay, captain!" He gave me an assist on the first goal, Nantes equalised, then I scored the winning goal. It was such an adrenaline shot.' For his part, the Portuguese was forced to book the table.

In autumn 2015 the elite of European football recruiters arranged to meet in Chile, where for a month the best juniors from around the world were to compete in the U-17 FIFA World Cup. During the tournament one player stood out. Victor Osimhen played all seven matches for the Golden Eaglets, reaching the final and showing the watching crowd what he could offer by scoring at least one goal in each game up until the showpiece conclusion. In the quarter final he led Brazil on a merry dance, left them groggy and dazed in a 3–0 victory. Not surprisingly, he netted in the all-African final the opening goal in a 2–0 win over Mali on the way to ending the competition as the Golden Boot winner with 10 goals.

The young striker from the Ultimate Strikers Academy was suddenly in the sights of some renowned teams. In January 2016 it was finally the German club VfL Wolfsburg that showed itself the most persuasive, and Victor James Osimhen arrived among the Wolves of Lower Saxony – although it took a year to finalise the deal. His beginnings were timid in the Bundesliga: between physical glitches and severe competition from Mario Gómez, Divock Origi and Bas Dost, the frail striker hardly played with the Greens across the Rhine and remained an unfulfilled talent. Loaned in the summer of 2018 to Sporting Charleroi, Osimhen found his feet and explosiveness and scored 12 times in 25 appearances.

During the following off-season, buoyed by his success over the border, LOSC recalled their man and he enjoyed a successful season among the Mastiffs. He immediately took apart two giants of the French game, scoring sumptuous doubles against both Nantes and Saint-Étienne. During this time he also made his debut in the UEFA Champions League. Unfortunately, the COVID-19 pandemic in the spring of 2020 curtailed Lille's championship push and Osimhen's progress, although in the truncated campaign he still managed to finish level at the top of the scoring charts with Neymar at PSG, on 13 goals each.

Purchased for €12 million, Lille sold their talented asset for six times the fee, a club-record fee of €80 million, to Napoli. There the bustling attacker became the darling of the Diego Armando Maradona Stadium, helping Napoli to the Scudetto. A tougher season followed before Osimhen, courted by several big clubs, surprisingly moved to Turkey, signing for Galatasaray for the 2024–25 season.

ENGLAND

Cole
PALMER

BORN: 6 May 2002, Manchester, England

HEIGHT: 1.89 m

POSITION: Attacking midfielder, winger

PROFESSIONAL CAREER: Manchester City FC, Chelsea FC

It's a celebration of thrills. When Cole Palmer scores the young England international rubs his biceps, hands in opposition as though to warm up. It's become his trademark every time he scores. On 15 April 2024 at the Stamford Bridge home of his club Chelsea, 'Cold' Palmer, as Chelsea fans have dubbed him, expressed himself in this way on a number of occasions after his incredible four-goal haul with the Blues in a 6–0 drubbing of Everton.

The Wythenshawe boy from the south of Greater Manchester was later voted by his peers as the best young player in England's prestigious top flight. To nearly everyone's surprise he had signed the previous summer for the London Blues of Chelsea despite having spent more than half his life in the Sky Blue of the Citizens of Manchester City.

Palmer joined Chelsea's academy at the age of eight and turned professional 10 years later. This left footer is by no means a monomaniac: he plays with his right foot with equal effectiveness when he has to. An old-fashioned playmaker or winger, he's also a specialist in firing in long-range shots that more often than not find the target. Here, again, his composure in front of goal confirms his nickname of Cold.

Manchester City's U-18 captain for the 2019–20 season, the teenager could have seen his dreams of top-level conquest come to a screeching halt as a teenager. At the age of 14 his long, lanky physique left some of the Citizens' talent scouts sceptical. One of them, the visionary Jason Wilcox, opposed his departure from the club: a wise decision. In October 2021 Cole made his Premier League debut against Burnley and on the same evening played for City's reserves – and scored a hat-trick!

A UEFA European champion at U-21 level in Georgia in July 2023, and with the English U-21 team winning the final against Spain 1–0, Palmer quickly got on the radar of the Three Lions senior team. Four months later his wish was granted: coach Gareth Southgate incorporated the phenomenon into his squad, and Palmer made his debut against Malta.

A symbolic transfer of power potentially followed. In the 61st minute of the 2–0 victory he replaced a Manchester United player, a certain Marcus Rashford: one Manchester lad replacing another. Palmer shone in limited playing time in the Euro 2024 tournament, netting as a substitute in the final against Spain although he was unable to help England claim the title.

DID YOU KNOW?

A huge Wayne Rooney fan as a child, Palmer spent his days wearing a red shirt on his shoulders – and, as his grandfather tells it, the kid didn't lose his fanaticism the first day he joined City U-8s. 'He was wearing a United shirt underneath his City one!' Palmer's grandfather revealed. For the Palmer family the choice of Manchester City made more sense because of the better welcome they received on their visit and the perfect facilities at West Gate.

SPAIN

PEDRI

BORN: 25 November 2002
Bajamar, Spain

HEIGHT: 1.74 m

POSITION: Midfielder

PROFESSIONAL CAREER:
UD Las Palmas,
FC Barcelona

This is the last little marvel of Spanish football! Pedro González López, aka Pedri, does not at first glance look like much. An introverted presence, he becomes formidable as soon as he enters a football pitch and teases the ball. After growing up in the Canary Islands, his native archipelago, the pocket magician first succeeded with the club of his village, UD Tegueste.

At just 15 years of age he joined the flagship team of Las Palmas. His rise was dazzling since it only took a few weeks to secure a professional contract there, and aged 16 years, 9 months and 25 days Pedri became the youngest scorer with the club. His progress might have been thwarted in February 2018 when the Canarian teenager completed a trial at Real Madrid that ultimately proved inconclusive.

Pumped up and back in Las Palmas, Pedri gave it his all in the Segunda Division while boosting the attacking style of his team. Whether in the long game, in small spaces or diagonal passes, Pedri knew how to do everything. Of great precision in his passing and endowed with an incomparable vision of the game, the Spanish elf amazed his coaches. 'Pedri has the quality of making things easier around him and seeing the game before others,' Pepe Mel commented.

With his devastating hooks, small stature and refined style, the Iberian Harry Potter was a star standout. By recruiting Pedri, Barça did not hide that the jewel of Tegueste inevitably recalled with his technical ease a certain Iniesta on his arrival at the Blaugrana training base. In October 2020 Pedri played his first classico, and even if Real Madrid came out on top winning 3–1 the impish maestro played up to the occasion and delivered some early examples of his burgeoning talent.

For the national team his progress was just as swift. He celebrated his first cap in March 2021 against Greece in a match that ended in a 1–1 draw, and three months later he became one of the revelations of the European Championships, a tournament that saw La Roja reach the semi-finals. After a gruelling first season – Pedri even played at the Tokyo Olympics – and despite a thigh injury that kept him out for a spell, away from the field the little genius signed an extension of his contract with Barça in October 2021 that tied him to the club until 2026. The exit clause was then set by the Catalan club at . . . €1 billion!

DID YOU KNOW?

In October 2020 during a UEFA Champions League match against the Hungarians of Ferencvárosi, which FC Barcelona won 5–1 at Camp Nou, Pedri scored his very first goal in the Barça jersey. Previously, Ansu Fati had also found the net. This was the first time in the history of the Catalan club that two players under the age of 18 had scored in the same European match.

ENGLAND

Jordan
PICKFORD

BORN: 7 March 1994, Washington, England

HEIGHT: 1.85 m

POSITION: Goalkeeper

PROFESSIONAL CAREER:
Sunderland AFC,
Darlington FC,
Alfreton Town FC,
Burton Albion FC,
Carlisle United FC,
Bradford City AFC,
Preston North End FC,
Sunderland AFC,
Everton FC

DID YOU KNOW?

The Merseyside derby between Liverpool and Everton makes him nervous. Two episodes have already marked the career of Jordan Pickford against the Reds. In December 2018 at Anfield the goalkeeper was caught out by an innocuous ball, and in the 96th minute he was beaten at close range by Divock Origi. The one-goal defeat was cruel for the Toffees. Almost two years later, this time at Goodison Park, Jordan's kamikaze outing caught Liverpool defender Virgil van Dijk and injured his right knee. Pickford escaped a red card as the Dutch defender was deemed offside.

When Jordan Pickford parried a penalty from Colombian Carlos Bacca in the Round of 16 of the World Cup 2018 in Moscow, he ended the curse. The hero of the Three Lions had ensured that England won a penalty shoot-out and squeezed into the quarter finals. They then progressed to the semi-finals, the first time they had travelled that far since Italia 1990.

It was the Everton goalkeeper, with just three caps to his name, who erased the memory of a succession of custodians who were unable to emerge from the shadows of their illustrious predecessors, world-class talents who patrolled between the posts such as Gordon Banks, Ray Clemence and Peter Shilton. Not bad for a 24-year-old boy with great maturity who never shirked responsibility. 'Nothing scares me,' Pickford admitted. 'Critics don't affect me; they can only make me better.'

Some observers spoke of arrogance, while others defended this very mobile goalkeeper with an exceptional left foot. His counterpart at Everton, the Dutchman Maarten Stekelenburg, pushed onto the bench by the little genius, willingly admitted it: 'Jordan knows what he is worth; he has great self-confidence,' he said. 'He works a lot and, above all, never panics. Nothing can fluster him.'

This appeared to be a logical continuation of a chaotic start to the journey to the top, a journey that saw six loans from Jordan's first club Sunderland to Darlington, Alfreton Town, Burton Albion, Carlisle United, Bradford City and Preston North End, clubs spread throughout the lower divisions of British football. From the Conference Premier to the championship, the kid from Sunderland had to grit his teeth to satisfy his passion.

When 'Speedy', as he is known, first walked onto the pitch he was placed in the goal because he was the biggest of the lot, and his brother Richard encouraged him to stay there. In an irony of fate his size was talked about 16 years later, during the World Cup. In the first round England cracked in front of the Belgian sharpshooters, and after the goal scored by the Red Devil's Adnan Januzaj, Pickford was criticised as being too short. He shook that off and now stands tall as an English giant.

In October 2025 Pickford signed a new four-year contract, committing to Everton until 2029.

BRAZIL

RAPHINHA

BORN: 14 December 1996, Porto Alegre, Brazil

HEIGHT: 1.76 m

POSITION: Winger

PROFESSIONAL CAREER: Vitória ES, Sporting CP, Stade Rennais FC, Leeds United, FC Barcelona

On his left arm Raphinha has a tattoo with these words 'Nunca foi sorte, sempre foi Deus' (It wasn't luck, it was God). On the pitch Raphael Dias Belloli, better known as Raphinha, dances a raging dance built on the cobblestones of a bumpy youth. The winger embodies the current Brazil, often where chaos reigns and talent emerges from the streets. However, the left-footed player from Porto Alegre almost never broke through. Born in the capital of Rio Grande do Sul, he grew up in a popular neighbourhood in a family where every real, the Brazilian currency, counts. 'There were days when I didn't have enough money to go to training,' he recalled.

Raphinha played barefoot in the streets, on the sand and on vacant lots, and at the age of 13 he joined the Avaí Academy but was not retained. Not having a plan B led to a series of matches for smaller Brazilian clubs because the big Brazilian clubs didn't want him, judging him too frail and too inconsistent.

One man did believe in him, though: Deco. The former maestro of FC Porto and Barcelona noticed Raphinha during an amateur tournament and integrated him into his network, allowing for a departure to Europe as he signed for Portuguese club Vitória de Guimarães. In 2018 after a sparkling season he signed for Sporting, where he scored and provoked but was still regarded as a squad player rather than a central part of the first team.

French club Rennes gambled and took him to Brittany for €21 million, and there Raphinha suddenly sprang into life. In Ligue 1 he shone brightly, daring with short dribbles that tormented defenders. A season later Marcelo Bielsa claimed him for Leeds United and shaped him into an end product. 'He taught me to think like a coach,' Raphinha commented, 'to run for others, to read the game instead of to endure it.' Under Bielsa, Raphinha became a constant thorn to Premier League defences and brought Elland Road to its feet.

Barcelona recruited him in 2022. At Camp Nou Raphinha discovered the complexity of a club under reconstruction and alternated flashes of brilliance with periods of self-doubt, but he never gave up. It culminated in a stellar 2024/25 season. 'What I've been through in my life has taught me how to fight,' he said. 'I don't give up, never.' Today he is a mainstay of the Barcelona squad and one of the leaders of a Brazilian Seleção aiming to reconquer the world under the guidance of Carlo Ancelotti.

DID YOU KNOW?

In the summer of 2022, when Leeds United accepted a colossal offer from Chelsea, Raphinha seemed remarkably close to signing for the London club. The deal was almost done, but behind the scenes the player was blocking the move. Ever since he had been a child he had dreamed of wearing the FC Barcelona jersey, and above all he promised his father that if he had the opportunity he would choose Barça at all costs. When the Catalan club finally entered the race with an offer lower than that of Chelsea, Raphinha kept his word and chose Barcelona against the advice of the agents and against financial logic.

ENGLAND

Marcus RASHFORD

BORN: 31 October 1997
Manchester, England

HEIGHT: 1.80 m

POSITION: Forward

PROFESSIONAL CAREER:
Manchester United FC,
Aston Villa FC (loan),
FC Barcelona (loan)

DID YOU KNOW?

In his very first league appearance at Old Trafford in February 2016, Marcus Rashford scored his first Premier League goal against Arsenal, a 3–2 win with a double to his credit. After these exploits the journalists rushed to talk to the new hero. To a reporter who asked him how he intended to celebrate the feat the young Red Devils forward, just 18 years old, answered full of confidence: 'I'm not going to celebrate anything. I have a chemistry test tomorrow!'

A pure-bred Mancunian, the young Marcus Rashford could easily have grown up at the Sky Blues but City training officials found him too weak. Taken to football matches from the age of six by older brother Dwain, the youngest Rashford discovered how fun the game was at the Fletcher Moss Rangers. Three years later Manchester United opened its doors and the kid from Wythenshawe, a popular area of Greater Manchester, flourished there until his adolescence.

Despite many clubs in the United Kingdom trying to lure him Marcus remained loyal to the Red Devils, and in the youth categories he accomplished amazing feats thanks in particular to a keen sense of goal. Outside the playing arena he came across as lacking assurance, but that was to change as he grew and became a major voice for social change in his homeland.

In early 2016, taking advantage of an avalanche of injuries up front, the English teenager was called into the first-team squad by Louis van Gaal for a debut in the Europa League against the Danes of FC Midtjylland. The slender striker was thrown into the Theatre of Dreams and scored a brace in a 5–1 victory. Aged 18 years and 117 days in his first professional outing, he became Manchester United's youngest goal scorer in European competition. He followed that up by netting a brace in his Premier League debut against Arsenal and scored the winner in his first Manchester derby, winning the hearts of supprters.

Before the European Championships in France he was called up to the England team as a potential partner to Harry Kane. After just three minutes of play during a warm-up match against Australia he slammed home his first goal in the Three Lions shirt. Despite his size Marcus impresses with his balance and sturdiness, fluidity around the attack, finesse in the pass and the power of his shooting. Excellent at hitting a clean strike on the run, Rashford made it one of his specialties.

He even made dead balls a part of his repertoire, scoring a glorious free kick against Wales at the 2022 FIFA World Cup in Qatar – one of three goals he scored during that tournament. But a tough season with Manchester United and a reported falling out with boss Rueben Amorim led to Rashford heading out on loan to Aston Villa in early 2025, then again at the start of the 2025–26 season on loan to FC Barcelona.

ENGLAND

Declan

RICE

BORN: 14 January 1999, Kingston upon Thames, England

HEIGHT: 1.88 m

POSITION: Midfielder

PROFESSIONAL CAREER: West Ham United FC, Arsenal FC

In the land of the Gunners Declan Rice is the gunner in chief! The midfielder underlined his brilliance in the quarter finals of the 2025 UEFA Champions League, where he scored two outlandish free kicks as Arsenal ousted the Spanish giants Real Madrid. Los Blancos are not likely to forget his impact on a nightmare evening at the Emirates Stadium any time soon! Rice was indeed the grain of sand that combusted Real's finely tuned machine that evening.

It all started for Rice in south-west London. At a noticeably young age he joined Chelsea's youth academy, but in 2014 at the age of 14 the club let him go. It was a harsh blow for the committed youngster. 'That day I cried a lot,' Rice said, 'but it gave me a strength that I didn't think I possessed.' Back to square one, West Ham United took a chance on the balletic ball player and it was a second opportunity Rice seized.

Rice made his professional debut at the age of 18, perhaps surprisingly given all that he went on to achieve, as a central defender. Very quickly, however, the Hammers' coaches saw something else in him: an ability to read the game and dictate the rhythm of a match. A shift into a defensive midfield role saw Rice become a natural leader and the soul of the team.

Capped by his country, he was just as essential. As England reached the final of the delayed European Championships in 2021, Rice was a midfield regular alongside Jude Bellingham. He represented a new generation of English player: talented, committed and structured. 'Playing for England is a huge source of pride,' Rice admitted, 'but it also brings pressure that you need to learn to transform into a strength.'

A string of solid seasons for West Ham followed, with the crowning glory coming in 2023 as Rice lifted the UEFA Europa Conference League trophy, the East London club's first piece of silverware since an FA Cup win in 1965. He was masterful in the win over Fiorentina in Prague, his last act as a Hammer being to lift the trophy aloft in front of the adoring fans.

It cost London rivals Arsenal €116 million to entice him to the Emirates, a price tag many doubted was worth it. However, it soon became apparent that Rice would be a key part of Mikel Arteta's system as he was a physical presence cutting out opposition counterattacks, was clean in the tackle and in possession and scored legendary goals.

DID YOU KNOW?

While some footballers associate numbers with their position or with nods to their family many are simply superstitious, and Declan Rice falls into this category. The Gunner has worn the number 41 since his years at West Ham's academy. As a teenager during a pre-season training camp in Seattle the club's steward entrusted him with the 41. Since then Declan Rice has always remained faithful to this number, and it could stay with him for the rest of his career. However, with the Three Lions he is forced to play with the number 4 in the national team for regulatory reasons.

SPAIN

RODRI

BORN: 22 June 1996
Madrid, Spain

HEIGHT: 1.9 m

POSITION: Defensive midfielder

PROFESSIONAL CAREER:
Villarreal CF,
Atlético de Madrid,
Manchester City FC

With a stroke of genius, Rodri delivered for an entire group and thus ensured the supreme coronation. The date 10 June 2023 will live long in football history, in particular the 68th minute of the UEFA Champions League final in Istanbul. After Manuel Akanji created an opening, Bernardo Silva managed to get to the byline. Inter Milan repelled the initial movement, but there was a major problem for the Nerazzurri: the ball found its way to Spanish maestro Rodri. We know the quality of the strike that followed from the Madrilenian of the Citizens who, from an instantaneous attempt, beautifully lodged the ball under the crossbar of the goal, leaving the Internazionale goalkeeper André Onana with little chance.

In making the breakthrough and ensuring the final success of a 1–0 victory, Rodrigo Hernández Cascante offered the big-eared cup to fans of Manchester City and a Pep Guardiola–inspired team that can finally be placed alongside the coach's former success at FC Barcelona. As for Rodri his 2022–23 season, already staggering with the double of the FA Cup and Premier League already in hand, was far from finished. Eight days later in Rotterdam, Rodri was omnipotent in the midfield of La Roja as he helped blow away the Nations League hopes of Croatia by winning the final 0–0 after extra time and 5–4 on penalties.

Often compared with Sergio Busquets for his ability to function as a rotating midfield anchor, the versatile Rodri possesses more power than his glorious elder. All defenders and goalkeepers notably fear his striking of the ball, even those who have seen it all before. Able to cover the whole field, the Castilian does not often need the support of his teammates to carry out his job. Recovery, relaunch, perceptive passing and shooting, he always relishes his capital role in the heart of the game and plays with a maturity and tactical sense that place him above his peers in that position.

Rodri plays just as metronomically with both feet, at a volume and pace that is much envied. The boy experienced a meteoric rise to such an extent that his teammates rely on his constant ability to be the dynamo around which the team's attacking style is built. Despite his new status as a star of European football, the Hispanic international does not want to change anything. If Pep Guardiola can legitimately be proud of his group – and as the treble winners why wouldn't he be? – the Catalan Rodri certainly remains one of the technician's finest discoveries.

DID YOU KNOW?

A real connection developed between the Spanish midfielder and Lucas and Théo Hernandez, the French internationals. When Rodri evokes their names in conversation he talks about his 'family'. The three players grew up together at Atlético's training centre Alcalá de Henares before they all departed on a different path, but always at the highest level. Their destiny appears to be intrinsically linked.

RODRYGO

BORN: 9 January 2001, Osasco, Brazil

HEIGHT: 1.74 m

POSITION: Winger, forward

PROFESSIONAL CAREER: Santos, Real Madrid Castilla, Real Madrid

DID YOU KNOW?

An avid skateboarder, Rodrygo is also an absolute fan of surfing and it's not unusual to see him in Nazaré, Portugal on one of the most legendary surf spots. Taking advantage of a rare day off, he didn't hesitate to travel 600 kilometres to attend the Nazaré Tow Surfing Challenge, which brings together the world's best extreme surfers.

To give you an idea of the potential of this Brazilian star, let's remember that Rodrygo Silva de Goes became the youngest Brazilian goal scorer in the history of the Copa Libertadores. In March 2018, in the colours of Santos FC, he scored a goal against Uruguay's Club Nacional in a 3–1 victory when he was aged just 17 years, two months and six days.

Three months later in the Brazilian championship Rodrygo hit a hat-trick against Vitória ES in a 5–2 thrashing. Despite approaches from Manchester City and PSG, Real Madrid won the race to sign him in 2018. In June 2019 he committed to the White House for six years with a transfer fee estimated at €45 million. One year later, in a memorable match against Inter Milan, the Nerazzurri had been holding their hosts to a 2–2 draw. With a magical finish to the game, the player already nicknamed 'El Rayo' delivered Real a prestigious success, netting the match winner.

In October 2019 Rodrygo was selected by Tite to start with the Brazil national team. He made his debut for the Seleção in a friendly in Riyadh against Argentina, during which he replaced Willian 20 minutes from the end. The Osasco native's first cap was a great achievement, vastly different from the player who had discreetly trained with Ceará SC in Fortaleza. Rodrygo's father, a former right back who became his agent, found him an agreement with Barcelona but Rodrygo finally opted for Real.

In May 2022 he achieved his first major breakthrough. In extra time in the UEFA Champions League against Manchester City Rodrygo scored twice to help Real qualify for the final, which they won a month later at the Stade de France against Liverpool 1–0. In autumn in Qatar the pill was harder to swallow: in the epilogue to the quarter final against Croatia, Rodrygo's part in the penalty shoot-out was a nightmare when the forward missed his effort.

Rodrygo's game is hard to define: he can play in multiple roles with impeccable versatility, a trait that enables him to play across the entire attacking front. He has few equals when it comes to getting into the gaps afforded by defenders, and if he sometimes suffers from his constant desire to do well even if he's spread himself too thin he's adamant about his roving brief. 'I've always said I'd rather prefer to play on the side,' he said. 'I don't like the role of centre forward.'

PORTUGAL

Cristiano

RONALDO

BORN: 5 February 1985
Funchal, Portugal

HEIGHT: 1.87 m

POSITION: Forward

PROFESSIONAL CAREER:
Sporting CP,
Manchester United FC,
Real Madrid CF,
Juventus FC,
Manchester United FC,
Al Nassr FC

DID YOU KNOW?

Arriving at the age of 12 in Lisbon, little Cristiano was expelled from his school after launching a chair at his teacher, who had made fun of the modest situation of his family and also of his accent. Born on the island of Madeira, despite tears of anger the boy was already showing a lot of character. Sports trainers quickly appreciated the kid's willingness to pull through the tough days.

It's the feeling of summer. At the beginning of July 2018, the conversations of football lovers invariably turned around the transfer window. After nine seasons at Real Madrid and the third Champions League in a row won in the jersey of the Merengues, Cristiano Ronaldo announced his departure for Juventus. The Portuguese star admitted to having been stunned by the standing ovation of the Piedmontese public after his incredible goal from an overhead kick during the UEFA Champions League quarter final in the spring against the Bianconeri. For €100 million, 'CR7' was heading for Turin.

Everywhere he has been the champion has always electrified the crowds and Juventus was no different, Ronaldo bagging goals aplenty before making an emotional return to Manchester United, the scene of his breakthrough onto the global stage as a worldwide phenomenon. A hard worker with the physique of an athlete, Cristiano exudes football.

Technically, he is unquestionably the best. With Lionel Messi he formed a duo of extraterrestrials and, as per the Argentinean, the Lusitanian broke record after record on the stadiums of world football. The latest? The Madeiran became the first player to win – unheard of – a league title in the three biggest championships in Europe: the English Premier League, Spanish Liga and Italian Serie A.

From Alex Ferguson to Manchester United to Zinedine Zidane at Real Madrid, his coaches have always installed him in the best conditions for him to best express his tremendous talent. To top it off, while Portugal has so far only gleaned a few international accolades, the child of Funchal led the Seleção to the supreme title at Euro 2016. Injured at the start of the final against the French team Ronaldo left his partners but, limping on the edge of the field and inhabited by such a desire to win, he transmitted this passion for victory to the whole group.

In 2003, when he was just 18 years of age, his training club, Sporting CP, played a friendly match against Manchester United. The United players were so stunned by the qualities of the young man that they eventually convinced Sir Alex Ferguson to recruit this future genius. This was the start of an extraordinary career that saw him become the highest goal scorer in men's international football history. Unfortunately for his legacy, his second spell at Old Trafford ended in an acrimonious exit and with a move to Al Nassr in Saudi Arabia.

GERMANY

Antonio
RÜDIGER

BORN: 3 March 1993, Berlin, Germany

HEIGHT: 1.9 m

POSITION: Centre back

PROFESSIONAL CAREER: VfB Stuttgart II, VfB Stuttgart, AS Roma (loan), AS Roma, Chelsea FC, Real Madrid

When he stepped up to convert the decisive spot kick at Etihad Stadium in April 2024 in the second leg of the Champions League quarter final against Manchester City, Antonio Rüdiger made Real Madrid's own fans nervous. The German defender is not renowned for being the best technician in the business, yet with determination he converted his attempt and sent the defending champions into oblivion. It took a good dose of courage and a certain aplomb to be one of the designated takers, because as he knew he would once again have incurred the wrath of the public had he missed.

Criticism has been a constant feature of his career, including when he won his first UEFA Champions League final with Chelsea in May 2021 in Porto, 1–0 against Manchester City. If he put Gabriel Jesus, Bernardo Silva, Raheem Sterling and Riyad Mahrez in their place, the most severe comments were unleashed after Antonio's violent intervention on Kevin De Bruyne. With a fractured nose, the Belgian had to leave his teammates on the hour mark.

A victim of racism in his youth and later in his career with AS Roma, Antonio Rüdiger has forged a strong character. Trained at a number of clubs in Berlin suburbs, including Tasmania, he joined the Borussia Dortmund academy as a teenager before completing his apprenticeship at VfB Stuttgart. He turned professional in 2012.

At the age of just 21 he celebrated his first cap for Germany in Hamburg, playing as a right back on his debut for the Mannschaft against Poland in an uninspiring 0–0 draw, but he missed Euro 2016 in France due to a torn knee ligament. Under Rudi Garcia and then Luciano Spalletti he discovered the rugged form he needed in the Italian championship with AS Roma.

In July 2017 he headed for London to sign a €35 million deal with Chelsea, where he found himself back with an Italian coach, Maurizio Sarri. When Frank Lampard succeeded Sarri on the bench Rüdiger lost his first-team status with the Blues, and it was not until the arrival of his compatriot Thomas Tuchel that he regained his place in a three-man defence. In the summer of 2022 Rüdiger moved to Real Madrid, where he has continued to flourish and silenced many of the doubters.

DID YOU KNOW?

Having just moved to Madrid with his family, Antonio Rüdiger had an incredibly special house-warming party. To celebrate their move the German defender was preparing a barbecue when the doorbell rang and the player found himself face to face with Carlo Ancelotti! 'I was very surprised. He sat down at our table, ate with us and met my family. He stayed for two hours, and we talked about everything. I'm honest: I've never experienced anything like it,' Rüdiger remembered.

ENGLAND

Bukayo

SAKA

BORN: 5 September 2001
Ealing, England

HEIGHT: 1.78 m

POSITION: Right winger

PROFESSIONAL CAREER:
Arsenal FC

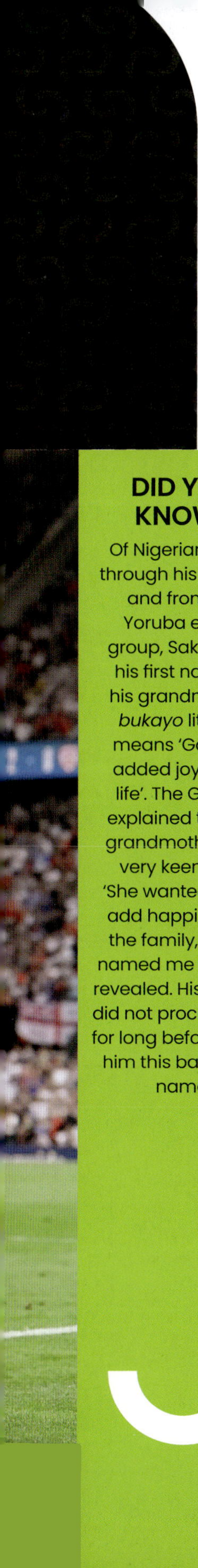

With his Brazilian appearance, the young Englishman precociously inherited a nickname that suited him perfectly: 'Sakinho'. With his swaying dribbles, the Gunners star excels at unseating an opposing defence and brings immediate danger in the final third. The fluidity of his gestures are amplified by a sharp technique, especially more impressive when the whole thing is done with speed and disconcerting execution.

Since his first excursion on the pitch with Watford, Saka has succeeded in everything he tried. He was only seven years old when he arrived at the Arsenal Academy Hale End, and his coaches were quickly convinced they had signed a star. A wonderful love story then began in the greater north London suburbs. Young Saka knows the notion of sacrifice, and in particular that he was not able to live like a normal teenager; in the Gunners training centre they do not mess around with the education of their future talents. While his football was inspired by local stars such as Thierry Henry, Dennis Bergkamp and Nwankwo Kanu, it was nevertheless a Swede who allowed him to take off. The youth coach at Arsenal, Fredrik Ljungberg, became the mentor for Saka, who was always listening and asking for advice.

In the 2019 off-season, while taking advantage of the absence in Arsenal's midfield of Aaron Ramsey and Alex Iwobi, the young winger was launched onto the big stage. Asked by the Nigerian Federation to link up with them, he declined the invitation of the Super Eagles and had only one objective: to shine with the English Three Lions. In October 2020 Saka was called by Gareth Southgate and earned his first cap in a friendly match against Wales at Wembley, a fixture that was won 3–0.

He returned to the temple of English football during Euro 2021 when England reached the final but, just like Marcus Rashford and Jadon Sancho, Bukayo Saka saw his penalty in the final shoot-out against Italy fail. Far from discouraging him, this ordeal reinforced the desire of the one Pierre-Emerick Aubameyang affectionately calls 'Little Chilli'. With confidence from coach at the Gunners Mikel Arteta, Bukayo Saka achieved a high standard during the 2022–23 season. Although Arsenal, long in the lead, was finally overtaken in the last straight by Manchester City in the title race, the hard-hitting Gunner had nothing to reproach himself for.

DID YOU KNOW?

Of Nigerian origin through his parents and from the Yoruba ethnic group, Saka owes his first name to his grandmother: *bukayo* literally means 'God has added joy to my life'. The Gunner explained that his grandmother was very keen on it: 'She wanted me to add happiness to the family, so she named me thus,' he revealed. His parents did not procrastinate for long before giving him this baptismal name.

EGYPT

Mohamed
SALAH

BORN: 15 June 1992
Nagrig, Egypt

HEIGHT: 1.75 m

POSITION: Forward

PROFESSIONAL CAREER:
Al Mokawloon Al Arab SC,
FC Basel, Chelsea FC,
ACF Fiorentina, AS Roma,
Liverpool FC

No one has forgotten that loose shoulder. In Egypt there was the nose of Cleopatra at the time of the pharaohs, and more than 20 centuries later there is Mohamed Salah's collarbone. Injured in a manly clash with Sergio Ramos in the Champions League final between Real Madrid and Liverpool in May 2018, the Egyptian striker almost missed the World Cup in Russia. Especially cruel was that it was Salah who carried his team almost single-handedly through qualification.

After a race against time Mohamed Salah returned to the group and even scored twice in the global competition, but Egypt's elimination was confirmed. It was obviously in Europe that 'Mo' had become a twinkling star. This space devourer who combined speed and skills had all the qualities of a spectacular player. This was a long way to travel for the child of Basyoun forced to change buses five times to reach Cairo when he went as a teenager with the Arab Contractors. It was a test that forged his character.

Rejected in 2011 by Zamalek, in Switzerland and at FC Basel more precisely Mohamed revealed himself. A transfer to Chelsea followed two years later, but he failed to establish himself at the forefront of the Blues' attack and featured in just 13 games over a two and a half year period at Stamford Bridge.

It was better in Italian Serie A, where the Egyptian expanded his footballing spectrum. At Fiorentina and then at Roma Salah he developed his tactical sense and, above all, became a much more efficient finisher, an area in which he had been deficient for a long time. Able to score goals off dazzling counterattacks from his own half of the field, the 'Pharoah' shone in the Italian capital before making a move to Liverpool.

Reds' boss Jürgen Klopp immediately fell in love with his new signing. 'Even if he doesn't score he is very useful because he stretches the opposing defences,' Klopp said. 'It opens spaces for my other attackers.' He had the nerves for the big occasion, as his second-minute penalty in the 2019 UEFA Champions League final against Tottenham Hotspur showed. It was the fastest-ever goal in a Champions League showdown. When Salah takes action it's usually all of Anfield that takes up the chorus of his anthem, to the tune of 'Sit Down' by James. With such talent, there are rarely any false notes.

DID YOU KNOW?

In 2018 during the elections in Egypt, Mohamed Salah could have been the challenger of the-then head of state, General el-Sisi. Indeed, to challenge the absence of a real opposition some Egyptian voters chose to slip the name of the football star into the ballot box. The Reds striker finished second in the ballot . . . without showing up! At the foot of the pyramids Salah was able to appreciate his immense popularity.

FRANCE

William SALIBA

BORN: 24 March 2001, Bondy, France

HEIGHT: 1.92 m

POSITION: Centre back

PROFESSIONAL CAREER:
AS Saint Étienne,
AS Saint Étienne B,
Arsenal FC,
OGC Nice (loan),
Olympique de Marseille (loan)

DID YOU KNOW?

Signed at US Bondy, the club in the city of his birth, at the age of six, William Saliba had as his coach in the U-11 team Wilfrid Mbappé, father of the current Real Madrid striker and captain of the France team Kylian. It is a period he has great memories of. 'He was my coach for one or two years. He was a real coach! He taught me everything, and if I am where I am today it is thanks to him.'

William Saliba is the calm player who every striker hates. They think they have the ball but he has already taken it. They think they have eliminated him from the game but he is always there. Small in stature in his youth, Saliba grew up in Bondy only a few streets away from Kylian Mbappé. Even as a youngster he always had one obsession: the ball.

At the age of 17 Saliba signed forms with Saint Étienne, where he began to play with disconcerting calmness for one of such tender years. Tall and slender, he was already impressing those in the know with his serenity. He played the game with no superfluous gestures and earned the nickname 'The Ice'.

After playing only a handful of matches for Saint Étienne, Arsenal pounced and snapped up the elegant defender for €30 million, but instead of throwing him into the deep end they loaned him out to learn his trade, first at Nice and then at Marseille. That's when it clicked: at Marseille Saliba played regularly and became an indispensable member of the team. In 52 matches for the French club he never once picked up a red card. Marseille coach Jorge Sampaoli was suitably impressed and became a big fan, heaping huge praise on Saliba.

A successful loan spell was always likely to see a swift return to the Emirates, with Mikel Arteta trusting Saliba by thrusting him into the action where he made the Arsenal defence a rock-like wall. In his debut against Crystal Palace he was voted player of the match and two weeks later he scored his first goal, sending a left-footed shot into the top corner against AFC Bournemouth. 'I closed my eyes and just hit it,' he said, smiling.

The 2023 campaign reminded Saliba that football can sometimes be harsh and that his body was fallible. A back injury kept him out, and in his absence Arsenal's chase for the Premier League title collapsed. It was then the consensus that Saliba was a pillar of the Arsenal defence was cemented.

At international level he was forced to wait, as French coach Didier Deschamps was observing his progress but felt he had some issues. Saliba was criticised for not being enough of a leader and for not being vocal enough. Far from offended, he worked doubly hard during team training at Clairefontaine and slowly got his rewards, finally establishing himself as an undisputed starter at the 2024 Euros in Germany. Now he is indispensable.

GERMANY

Leroy
SANÉ

BORN: 11 January 1996
Essen, Germany

HEIGHT: 1.83 m

POSITION: Forward

PROFESSIONAL CAREER:
FC Schalke 04,
Manchester City FC,
FC Bayern Munich,
Galatasaray SK

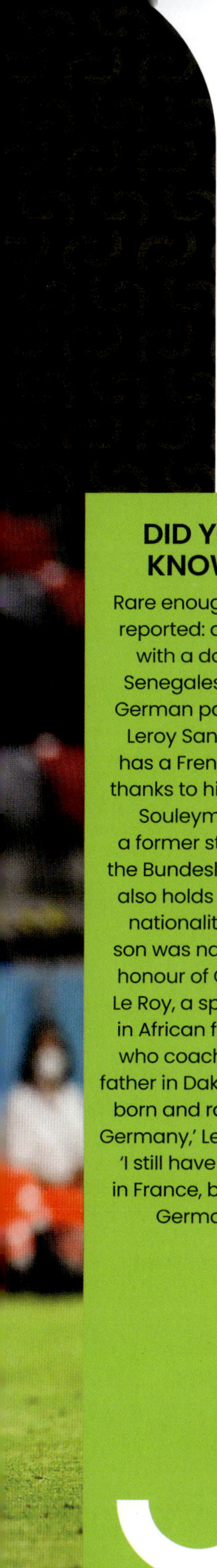

SANÉ

What possessed German national team manager Joachim Löw to deprive himself of Leroy Sané for the World Cup in Russia in 2018? In his list, the one who had just been crowned champion of England with Manchester City and author of a rich season of Premier League exploits was conspicuous by his absence. To everyone's surprise 'Jogi' preferred Julian Brandt. Admittedly, the failure of Germany and their first-round elimination were not due just to the absence of the stirring kid from the Ruhr, but all the same his omittance was a surprise.

Already during Euro 2016 in France German supporters had complained about the lack of playing time granted to this great Ronaldinho fan. Thus, during the semi-final loss against France in Marseille at 0–2 the future Citizen had only come onto the field in the last quarter of an hour. However, a few weeks previously while in the jersey of Schalke 04 he had accomplished a mind-blowing performance against Real Madrid in the Champions League.

Elusive, the young winger had driven the Spanish defenders to distraction. During the second leg of the Round of 16 fixture the German club achieved an incredible result by winning 4–3 at the Santiago-Bernabéu Stadium. Too bad for Schalke and Leroy Sané, the Merengues won 2–0 in the first leg to oust the team from Gelsenkirchen.

Already experienced in European games at the age of 20, Sané continued his apprenticeship in the Champions League with Manchester City. His performances down the flank for the Citizens pleased his boss Pep Guardiola, even if Guardiola reproached him occasionally for his lack of consistent effort and a certain propensity to drift away from his assigned position.

An interesting aside saw Sané cost a punter a tidy sum in 2017. In a Champions League elimination tie against AS Monaco at the Etihad Stadium the German arrow netted the final goal in a 5–3 success and thus deprived the poor punter of a winning ticket. For €2 the punter in question had bet on City to win 4–3, and that goal cost a win of €34,200! Sané heard about the unfortunate incident and tweeted an apology. 'I read that in the newspapers . . . Sorry for the poor guy,' he posted after the match.

Sané made his national team debut in 2015 and went on to reach a half century of caps at the 2022 FIFA World Cup in Qatar. In June 2025 he signed with Galatasaray.

DID YOU KNOW?

Rare enough to be reported: already with a double Senegalese and German passport, Leroy Sané also has a French one thanks to his father Souleymane, a former striker in the Bundesliga who also holds French nationality. The son was named in honour of Claude Le Roy, a specialist in African football who coached his father in Dakar. 'I was born and raised in Germany,' Leroy said. 'I still have family in France, but I feel German.'

PORTUGAL

Bernardo

SILVA

BORN: 10 August 1994
Lisbon, Portugal

HEIGHT: 1.73 m

POSITION: Attacking midfielder, right winger

PROFESSIONAL CAREER: SL Benfica, AS Monaco, Manchester City FC

Heading for Seixal, where the Benfica training centre is located, youth coach Fernando Chalana equipped his protégé, none other than Bernardo Silva, with an evocative nickname: 'Messizinho' (little Messi). Of incredible vivacity and unequalled skill, the child nevertheless had difficulty standing out from the crowd in the initial stages. 'At this period of my life physique mattered a lot, and I was really very little,' the Portuguese will-o'-the-wisp recalled. At Benfica the standards were exceedingly high and they placed an emphasis on strength, meaning that despite everything the gateway to the first team remained stubbornly locked for Silva. 'I trained finally with the pro group but as a left back,' Silva said, 'so I understood that I had no future at Benfica.'

Then manager at the Lisbon Eagles Jorge Jesus just did not believe in his clever schemer, considering him too small to progress. 'He thinks faster than he is short,' Hélder Cristóvão, his B-team coach, assured. Only one option remained for this relentless person who, despite a lack of playing time, did not give up and secured a loan move to an ambitious club, joining up with AS Monaco in the 2014 off-season. He was barely at the Principality club before they exercised the right to purchase him from his parent team.

Leonardo Jardim felt it was the right move: 'Bernardo creates huge problems for an opposing defence thanks to his movement. He is also important in the transition phase as well as in the construction of our moves.' When the Portuguese schemer was deployed in an off-centre role to better fit into the system his elegant touches off the left foot were a feast for the eyes. Unpredictable in his choices, Bernardo Silva became an essential pawn of an AS Monaco team that stubbornly shook off the challenge of PSG and was crowned Champions of France in 2017.

Silva's guilty pleasure was holding on to possession, something that led to him being considered ripe for a bigger club. 'I often joked with him, saying that he was a player made for Barça,' João Tralhão, who also managed him at Benfica, recalled. It was not Barcelona but Pep Guardiola's Manchester City that stole him away from the south of France. He went on to land that historic treble in 2023, creating and scoring with abandon in a superb City set-up. It was a wonderful case of revenge for the frail toddler who has grown into the main man.

DID YOU KNOW?

On the evening of the elimination of the Champions League semi-final against Real Madrid in 2022, the Portuguese international admitted to a Madrid player his desire to play for Real: 'Tell Florentino to sign me; I want to play here!' Silva allegedly said. Bernardo loved the atmosphere at the Santiago Bernabéu and was potentially after a change of scenery. The following season the teams reconvened in the Champions League when Real again met City at the semi-final stage, and it was the star performance of the Portuguese that single-handedly eliminated the title holders!

SOUTH KOREA

Heung-min

SON

BORN: 8 July 1992
Chuncheon-si, South Korea

HEIGHT: 1.83 m

POSITION: Forward

PROFESSIONAL CAREER:
Hamburger SV,
Bayer 04 Leverkusen,
Tottenham Hotspur FC

DID YOU KNOW?

On the football stock exchange he is among the most bankable assets in the game. The South Korean Son Heung-min has become one of the most expensive and valuable pieces on the chessboard of world football: his transfer in 2015 to Tottenham for €30 million was one of the highest fees paid for a player of Asian origin. At the age of 27 the forward some journalists nicknamed 'Sonaldo' for his sense of goal and explosiveness is a real star from Seoul.

To escape the obligations of military service in his country Son Heung-min found the right vein of form. In South Korea some champions are exempt from donning fatigues and carrying a rifle if they land medals of global importance, and during the summer of 2018 the Asian striker took up the challenge: that of participating with Korea's U-21 selection in the Asian games.

On Indonesian soil the champion forward led the young South Koreans to the final, during which they dominated Japan and claimed a 2–1 success in extra time. If placed it would have been a successful bet, and Son returned home with a winner's medal around his neck that saved him from the obstacle course, push-ups and guard towers!

From an early age the boy had always known how to adapt and discovered football in hardly encouraging circumstances. Punished by his father, the young Taeguk warrior was told to learn to tame a leather ball. Intoxicated by long minutes of juggling, the 10 year old learned the skills required to dominate that sphere. He was just a teenager barely out of his cocoon when he joined the Hamburg training centre. At a young age and thrust into a different culture, for young Son this was like living on a different planet.

'I didn't know anyone,' the dyed in the wool South Korean admitted. 'I thank all the great players for saying a word to me when I needed support. For example, Rafael van der Vaart and Ruud van Nistelrooy were helpful for me in Hamburg.' In the Bundesliga Son quickly became a phenomenon, and his express pace and determination to push his actions to the end seduced the media and spectators.

His debut in the Champions League drew a sizeable audience back home in his native country. 'At kick-off, it was five o'clock in the morning in Seoul and they were all up watching,' a visibly moved Son said. 'I felt like I owed them something, [that] it's my responsibility to play well.' Hence the diligent hours of training and the stubbornness to never let an opportunity pass him by. After a timid debut season at Tottenham, to whom he switched in 2015 from Bayer 04 Leverkusen, Son became better than a stand-in for Harry Kane. He instead created one of the great Premier League partnerships, the Son–Kane double act – a vital part of Tottenham's progression to the 2019 Champions League final.

GERMANY

Marc-André

TER STEGEN

BORN: 30 April 1992
Mönchengladbach,
Germany

HEIGHT: 1.87 m

POSITION: Goalkeeper

PROFESSIONAL CAREER:
Borussia Mönchengladbach,
FC Barcelona

Marc-André ter Stegen, who became the seventh German player to play for FC Barcelona when he joined their powerful squad in the summer of 2014, entered the Catalan monument on tiptoes. The reason for this was he was leaving Germany and entering the unknown.

The young Rhenish stopper had just spent 18 years at Borussia Mönchengladbach, the club of his hometown, which practically adopted him from out of the crib. In April 2011, at just 19 years of age, the intrepid, uninhibited goalkeeper was offered a chance to start in the Bundesliga thanks to the flair of Lucien Favre, then in charge of the Foals – the nickname given to Gladbach players.

Marc-André amazed the local public with his prowess on his line and allowed his team to gain confidence. It was little surprise, then, that when he got a standing ovation on his final game with Borussia 'Marco' cracked and could not hold back the tears.

He arrived in Catalonia with a big challenge: replace Victor Valdés, who had just played 535 games in the Blaugrana jersey. It was, however, a curious first season in the Camp Nou side: he did not play a match in La Liga, as it was the Chilean Claudio Bravo who was favoured for league action. Marco was established in the Spanish Cup side but also, and more importantly, in the Champions League set-up. With a record 13 outings to his credit in the Champions League, the young German goalkeeper lifted the trophy after Barça's 3–1 victory against Juventus.

Despite this flashy career and more than honest beginnings, support for the goalkeeper in the Rhineland was not unanimous. This situation did not panic him, though; time would be his best ally. For his debut with the national team during the 2012–13 season, Marc-André lost in his first three matches: against Switzerland 3–5, Argentina 1–3 and then the United States 3–4. An extremely rare feat for a German international!

He ended up convincing even the most sceptical, and with his calm presence he became an essential piece in the Catalan system and for the national team. At the start of the 2022–23 season he had amassed four La Liga titles and five Copa Del Rey trophies to add to his Champions League gong.

DID YOU KNOW?

Interviewed by the Spanish daily *El País*, Marc-André ter Stegen did not hide the fact that his environment hardly interested him. 'People laugh when I tell them that I have no thoughts about football,' he revealed. 'Sometimes they ask me the name of a player during a TV broadcast, and I have no idea. I remember better his movements, his way of standing out, than his name.' Each to his own, of course!

FRANCE

Marcus
THURAM

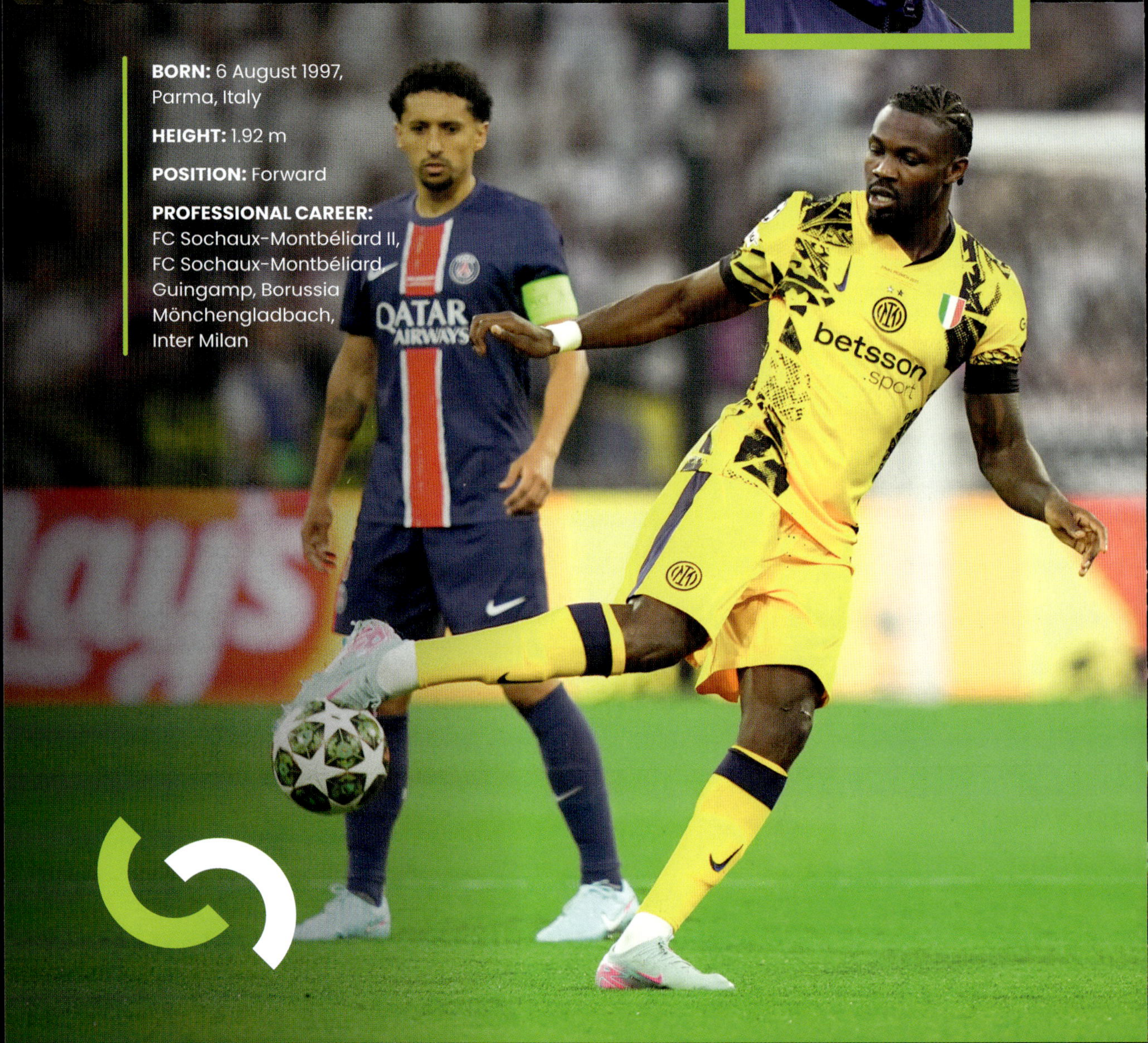

BORN: 6 August 1997, Parma, Italy

HEIGHT: 1.92 m

POSITION: Forward

PROFESSIONAL CAREER:
FC Sochaux-Montbéliard II, FC Sochaux-Montbéliard, Guingamp, Borussia Mönchengladbach, Inter Milan

DID YOU KNOW?

Like his father, Marcus Thuram is very committed to the fight against racism. His first name is a tribute to Marcus Garvey, a Jamaican activist of the early 20th century who was an inspiration for Pan-Africanism, a movement to unite Africans and their descendants outside Africa. After the death in the United States of George Floyd, Thuram celebrated a goal by taking a knee, a gesture that has become a symbol to denounce police violence. It is a cause that is close to his heart, as well as to that of his father.

THURAM

The son of a world champion: this is what was said about Marcus Thuram at the beginning of his career. Marcus is still Lilian's son, but the times have changed. The famous defender, who scored twice in the semi-finals of the 1998 World Cup, is on his way to becoming known as the father of Marcus!

History was taking shape at Sochaux, where there was no preferential treatment. At the age of 18 he got a taste of Ligue 2. Not yet a fearsome goal scorer, he was used out wide as a winger. There was no immediate spark but in every possession of the ball there was a surge of expectation, an underlying current that was easy to see, and always the constant desire to not just be the son of . . . 'At Sochaux I learned to fight,' was his summation.

Next came Guingamp. The club believed in him and Marcus was transformed, gaining muscle, volume and character. In the 2019 Coupe de la Ligue it was his goal, a decisive penalty in the 92nd minute, that eliminated Paris Saint-Germain at the Parc des Princes. He took his moment with clarity, showing no nerves, and that evening the followers of football in France began to think that Thuram was emerging from his father's shadow.

By this stage Thuram was already aiming elsewhere. He chose Germany, where Borussia Mönchengladbach welcomed him, and there he exploded. In his first German Cup match he scored a double, and in the Bundesliga he became a safe bet that attracted attention. Inter Milan offered him a chance in Serie A.

When he arrived at the San Siro Thuram slotted into an amazing collective. His contribution? Thirteen goals and an equal number of assists as the team raced to the League title. The icing on the cake for Thuram was the award for the goal of the season. At the Giuseppe Meazza he has succeeded in making people forget the Lu-La, the partnership of Romelu Lukaku and Lautaro Martínez, and has earned his place in the hearts of the supporters.

'Tikus' (Thuram's nickname) was playing the best football of his career in Lombardy but was slow to translate that form into the French national team. Although he worked hard and was unselfish and a diligent trainer, he faced a series of frustrating performances. Eventually, persistence paid off and he finally broke his goal drought with the national team, netting against Ireland in 2023. Didier Deschamps was never worried, though, and retains full confidence in the forward.

SPAIN

Ferran

TORRES

BORN: 29 February 2000
Foios, Spain

HEIGHT: 1.84 m

POSITION: Forward

PROFESSIONAL CAREER:
Valencia CF,
Manchester City FC,
FC Barcelona

DID YOU KNOW?

As his Instagram account testifies, Ferran Torres loves dogs: for more than 10 years he shared his daily life with Minnie, Lluna and Milo. A nature lover and sensitive to animal causes, he was committed during his English stay to help with the British charity association Wild at Heart, a foundation whose mission is to save abandoned and abused dogs.

From Paris, Lionel Messi must have choked on seeing the money paid for Ferran Torres by Barça! For €55 million Ferran became the most expensive Spanish signing in the Catalan club's history.

Born into football in Valencia and educated in England by Pep Guardiola in Manchester, Torres arrived in Barcelona with a sign on his back as the announced saviour. Barça was in full reconstruction mode, and fellow Spaniard Xavi arrived on the bench of the club he served in the role of firefighter. On Xavi's list of players to recruit, the City striker was at the very top. This was a return to the country where he made his debut, for Valencia, at only 17 years of age.

He played almost 100 matches in the colours of the Blanquinegros, but the Valencian club was in need of cash and let him slip away for €25 million to Manchester City. The new star of Spanish football scored 16 goals in his first season in the United Kingdom. On the wing life was better, even if his dribbling profile as that of a soloist on one side was undermined by Guardiola.

Repositioned as a false 9 by his coach, Torres adapted and continued his good performances. His versatility and mind proved to give sacred added value, but City had rich problems and a plethora of attackers in his position. The siren call of Barça did the rest. Xavi wanted Ferran and the Spanish striker dreamed of writing the post-Messi history at the Blaugrana club.

In the national team La Roja was counting on him to find his true colours. The youngest player in history to reach 10 goals in the Spanish jersey at 21 years and 192 days, better than Raúl González at 21 years and 277 days or Fernando Torres at 22 years and 79 days, Ferran applied for the position of leader at the forefront of the Spanish attack.

He was the type of goal scorer capable of netting a hat-trick against Germany in a 6–0 win in only his seventh cap. He was the first to achieve this feat against the Germans since England front man Michael Owen had done so in 2001. Any resemblance to the Reds' pocket striker ends there – or perhaps it doesn't. Lifting a Ballon d'Or is not a given for any player, but Ferrán Torres does not rule out anything. There has been the Spain of Fernando Torres, and there is a good chance there will soon be a Ferrán Torres's Spain.

BELGIUM

Leandro
TROSSARD

BORN: 4 December 1994, Maasmechelen, Belgium

HEIGHT: 1.72 m

POSITION: Winger, forward

PROFESSIONAL CAREER: KRC Genk, Lommel SK (loan), KVC Westerlo (loan), OH Leuven (loan), Brighton & Hove Albion FC, Arsenal FC

DID YOU KNOW?

The Arsenal supporter American actor Anne Hathaway made no secret of her admiration for Leandro Trossard. In April 2024 in the midst of promoting her new film *The Idea of Being You*, directed by Michael Showalter, the actor was backstage at a Premier League match in which Arsenal were playing Wolverhampton. Just before half-time the Belgian winger opened the scoring for the Gunners, prompting Hathaway to exclaim 'Oh, I love you!' Arteta's men eventually prevailed 2–0.

Beyond simply his resemblance to French international referee Clément Turpin, Belgian Leandro Trossard has made a name for himself in England and especially since his move to Arsenal. By March 2023 he had achieved three assists in the same season, a feat he was able to accomplish in the same match with the Gunners at Fulham, tearing apart the Cottagers in a 3–0 win. This came off the back of a hat-trick five months earlier, this time with Brighton against Liverpool in an epic 3–3 draw.

In January 2023 in search of a creative midfielder Arsenal had set their sights on the winger, signing him on a three and a half year contract and with an estimated transfer price of around €30 million. The following month the new Gunner found the net against Brentford in a 1–1 draw. To Mikel Arteta's great satisfaction, Trossard's influence on the game was immediately felt. His role as, in modern parlance, a 'nine and a half' suited the Spanish coach.

The native of Maasmechelen completed his youth training at KRC Genk, where he turned professional in 2012 even though he was still underage. However, he was soon loaned out before moving on to Lommel, Westerlo and Leuven. His return to Genk was a success, as he played in the Belgian Cup final in 2018 – a defeat by Standard de Liège, 0–1 after extra time – before winning the Jupiler Pro League title the following season.

The following summer Leandro soared over the channel to become a Seagull for Brighton & Hove Albion. With the confidence of his coach Graham Potter he quickly made his mark with the Seagulls, with whom he won his first international cap in a European qualification fixture. In September 2020 national coach Roberto Martínez launched him into the rich history of the Red Devils in Copenhagen during a 2–0 win over Denmark.

For Arsenal Trosard enjoyed a monumental 2023–24 season, playing with regularity and putting in first-rate performances in the Gunners' midfield as well as netting some decisive goals. It's just a shame that in the home straight Arsenal were overtaken by Manchester City, narrowly missing the club's 14th Premier League title.

FRANCE

Dayot

UPAMECANO

BORN: 27 October 1998, Évreux, France

HEIGHT: 1.86 m

POSITION: Centre back

PROFESSIONAL CAREER:
FC Liefering, FC Red Bull Salzburg, RB Leipzig, Bayern Munich

DID YOU KNOW?

French international Dayot Upamecano revealed that he worked on his voice, not to sing but to better direct his defence. Working on his vocal cords helped Upamecano communicate better. 'When I was young I had difficulty making myself heard,' he revealed. 'This is nothing new, but I felt the need to work on my voice. We collaborated with an opera professional. Those were a bit complicated words to repeat. The idea is to do it with a strong voice so that it carries, for 90 minutes. We sang too.' Next step for Upamecano might be a blind audition in *The Voice*!

Singing rap in the city of Madeleine in Évreux or listening to the concerts of Mozart in Salzburg, Dayot Upamecano has made a big leap in life, and not just musically. In only a few short years the timid teenager became, first in Austria and then Germany, one of the world's best defenders. A player who resembles the great French star Marcel Desailly was not even 17 years of age when he seduced the RB Salzburg recruiters and learned his trade alongside Naby Keïta before Keïta's transfer to Liverpool.

Originally from Guinea-Bissau, he inherited his first name of Dayotchanculle from his grandfather's former village. He got his first taste of football at the Vaillante d'Angers, where some volunteers had already noticed his consistent ball touch while he was still a child. 'I wasn't the best, but I would never stop running!' Upamecano admitted.

From the age of 10 Dayot grew up in the training facility of Valenciennes after initially starting with the juniors in Évreux. Already equipped with an impressive range of skills and the ability to play in a number of positions, the teenager was in the crosshairs of many clubs who coveted his ability. A trip across the channel saw him visit with Manchester United, but the English club was unable to offer any educational or sporting guarantees.

In July 2015, supported by his parents, Dayot opted for Red Bull Salzburg, immediately being loaned to the franchise's sister club FC Liefering. It was the start of a productive spell in the Red Bull system, with Upamecano moving back to Salzburg to play 21 matches in total, including five in the UEFA Champions League.

In January 2017 he made the switch from one Red Bull to another, signing for RB Leipzig in the German Bundesliga. It wasn't long before he became one of the best central defenders in the league, and he continued his rise by switching to giants Bayern Munich for a hefty transfer fee.

Having made his senior international debut in September 2020 in a UEFA Nations League group stage match with Sweden, Dayot bagged a maiden international goal against Croatia before becoming a regular in the team that came so close to FIFA World Cup glory in Qatar 2022. After the international retirement of Raphaël Varane, Les Bleus have certainly found their new boss in defence!

URUGUAY

Federico
VALVERDE

BORN: 22 July 1998
Montevideo, Uruguay

HEIGHT: 1.82 m

POSITION: Midfielder

PROFESSIONAL CAREER:
CA Peñarol, Real Madrid CF, Deportivo de La Coruña, Real Madrid

DID YOU KNOW?

In January 2020 during the Real–Atlético Spanish Super Cup final clash played in Saudi Arabia, Federico Valverde was having a funny evening. After a desperate tackle against Álvaro Morata, the Uruguayan was sent off as the last defender. His team still won, 4–1 on penalties after the game had ended 0–0 after extra time, and Valverde was named as Man of the Match!

The legend is tenacious and the image sticks in the memory of Federico Santiago Valverde Dipetta. At the start of his life, even when he was barely able to stand up, he was already running after a ball. He joined the Danube Academy in the Uruguayan capital, Montevideo, but even with proper registration the toddler was too small to play official matches. After being introduced to the watching crowd because he looked like a mascot, Little Valverde took off his metaphorical diaper and played anyway in a friendly game in which he scored a goal.

His nickname was profound: 'El niño del panal' (the child in a diaper). He was not even six years of age and already had a good reputation.

Inevitably, after impressing locally the fact that he made the move to Peñarol, the country's flagship club, was no surprise. Despite his introverted side the young man oozed modern football and his rise became dazzling. In the summer of 2016, for just €5 million, Real Madrid sets its sights on the little wonder who enchanted in the middle of the field. A complete player, Valverde is as good at creating openings for others as he is sealing defensive breaches.

Always invaluable in transition phases, he feels at ease everywhere on a field. As for his ability to find penetrative passes, the young Uruguayan has hardly any equivalent. After his debut with the Merengues reserve at La Castilla, Federico went on loan for a season at Deportivo La Coruña to toughen up.

As soon as he returned to the capital, during the 2018–19 season, El Niño immediately seduced Julen Lopetegui and then Santiago Solari, who followed one another on the Real Madrid bench. However, it was during the following term that Valverde took on a new dimension in a squad headed by Zinedine Zidane, a player whom the Uruguayan prodigy worshipped. The French coach had Valverde as the first name on the team sheet when he prepared his roster for matches. The kid had turned the hierarchy, however well established, upside down at Real.

After being awarded the Silver Ball at the 2017 U-20 World Cup, a tournament that convinced Real of his worth, Valverde made his senior debut in August of the same year and went on to become a regular selection for La Celeste.

THE NETHERLANDS

Virgil
VAN DIJK

BORN: 8 July 1991
Breda, The Netherlands

HEIGHT: 1.95 m

POSITION: Defender

PROFESSIONAL CAREER:
FC Groningen, Celtic FC,
Southampton FC,
Liverpool FC

DID YOU KNOW?

For €84 million, Virgil van Dijk signed with Liverpool on 27 December 2017. Transferred from Southampton, the Dutchman thus became at that time the most expensive defender in the history of football. In the standings he was ahead of two Frenchmen: Aymeric Laporte and Benjamin Mendy, both recruited by Manchester City. Like some of the stars of Dutch football such as Frank Rijkaard or Ruud Gullit, the Liverpool defender is of Surinamese origin through his mother.

With only a few titles gleaned in Scotland, Virgil van Dijk came to the Reds to fill his cupboard with trophies, and he came so close in the Premier League in May 2019 when his Liverpool side went neck and neck with Manchester City in the title race. With the Citizens racking up 98 points to seal the title against Liverpool's 97, the pill was hard to swallow. Fortunately, the epilogue in the Champions League had a much more favourable outcome for the Dutchman and his teammates, winners of the final against Tottenham Hotspur.

When he arrived at Anfield in the winter of 2018, van Dijk did not imagine that his signing would become a political issue. The cost of the fee was a bone of contention and especially with José Mourinho, then coach of Manchester United. 'Our competitors are buying defenders at the cost of attackers,' Mourinho bemoaned. His German counterpart at Anfield, Jürgen Klopp, warmed the spirits of van Dijk when he replied to the Portuguese coach's grumbles. 'We don't set the prices; it's the market,' was Klopp's rejoinder.

Far from all these controversies, Virgil quickly melded into the Liverpool collective. In his role as a towering centre back 'Vig' has few equals. He works standing up, never throwing himself at the feet of an adversary, and anticipates actions before they take place. Obviously, with his stature his aerial game borders on perfection. With an excellent passing range, the Dutchman does not hesitate to take risks to find his attackers.

The only question from Reds fans when he arrived at Liverpool was his perceived inexperience. His career up to that point had taken in Groningen in his homeland, Glasgow Celtic and Southampton, decent clubs but not of the stature of Liverpool. Charismatic and determined, van Dijk adapted well to European evenings and high-tempo encounters against the English Big Five, leading his team to the title in 2019–20 and banishing memories of the year before.

Since his debut with the Netherlands in 2014 he has been a mainstay of the Oranje defence and their return to prominence in international football, and the colossus of Breda is no stranger to the Dutch revival. It was van Dijk who, in equalising in stoppage time against Germany – the match ending 2–2 – who sent Ronald Koeman's team into the four-team Nations League finals at the expense of France in 2019.

PORTUGAL

VITINHA

BORN: 13 February 2000, Santo Tirso, Portugal

HEIGHT: 1.72 m

POSITION: Midfielder

PROFESSIONAL CAREER: FC Porto B, FC Porto, Wolverhampton Wanderers (loan), Paris Saint-Germain FC

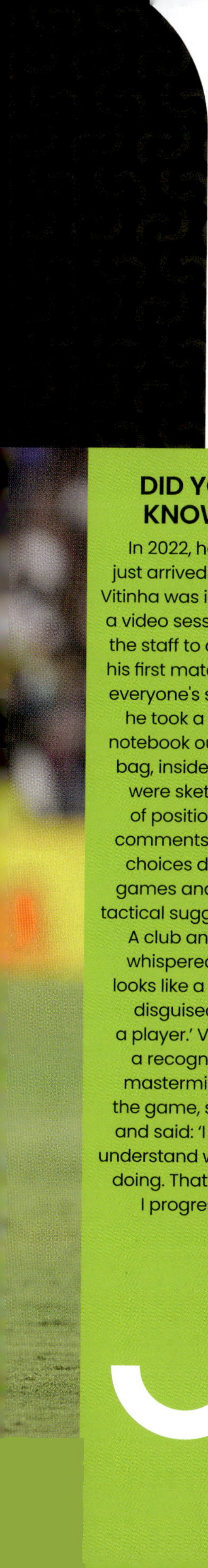

DID YOU KNOW?

In 2022, having just arrived at PSG, Vitinha was invited to a video session with the staff to analyse his first matches. To everyone's surprise he took a small notebook out of his bag, inside which were sketches of positioning, comments on his choices during games and even tactical suggestions. A club analyst whispered: 'He looks like a coach disguised as a player.' Vitinha, a recognised mastermind of the game, smiled and said: 'I like to understand what I'm doing. That's how I progress.'

Vitinha is the anti-star in a club of stars. He plays it simple, short and neat as though he had a debt to repay, transforming attacks with shrewd movements and playing geometrically perfect balls. On the pitch he thinks faster than everyone else, already being at the next pass while others are still making their decision.

Born in Santo Tirso in 2000, Vitinha grew up at Porto with a simple dream to play for FC Porto as his father had done. He entered the academy at the Portuguese club early as a small, frail child and was often overlooked because of his physique. 'I was told that I wouldn't go far,' he admitted, 'but I knew what I had in my feet.'

In 2020 he started with the professionals but he wasn't there for long. Wolverhampton Wanderers in the Premier League came calling and took the diminutive midfielder on loan. However, while in England Vitinha hardly played, perhaps being too lightweight for the English top flight. He returned to Porto with his head held high, and there he burst into life. In every match he had close to 100 touches, organising and building the game, and he became the master of the field.

Vitinha arrived in Paris in 2022, signing on the dotted line for Paris Saint-Germain. In his first season doubts persisted, with many thinking he was too sporadic. Then, slowly, it all changed: not in the physical aspect of the player, but in his head. His performances matured, there was little fuss in each display and the boss, Luis Enrique, not one to freely give out compliments, began to call him his totem.

The Spaniard installed Vitinha into his golden triangle in the middle of the PSG team, with the result that Vitinha was on fire. PSG had long been searching for a player who could boss the game, taking it by the scruff of the neck. His best assets are that he can play for 90 minutes with lucidity, run 10 kilometres per game but always with intelligent running, and that he nearly always makes the right choice in possession.

His 2024–25 season could have made him a serious contender for the Ballon d'Or, but he's not concerned about awards. Instead, he is already focused on improving his game, becoming a world reference for his position. PSG and Portugal can rest easy, for Vitinha is not after personal glory: he just wants to play and exploit his talent to the full.

SERBIA

Dušan

VLAHOVIĆ

BORN: 28 January 2000
Belgrade, Serbia

HEIGHT: 1.90 m

POSITION: Forward

PROFESSIONAL CAREER:
Partizan Belgrade,
ACF Fiorentina,
Juventus FC

The Old Lady did not hesitate to break her piggy bank to snap up the striker, spending nearly €80 million in the middle of winter 2021 – a record for the mid-season transfer window. It is true that the goal scorer's figures were enough to turn the heads of the Juventus board in Turin: 49 goals and 8 assists in 108 games at Fiorentina, which ranked him as a serious Serie A striker. Now the Serbian was installed at the top of the Bianconeri attack, with the famous number 7 on his back and in the position once inhabited by Cristiano Ronaldo.

Born on 28 January 2000, Vlahović twice offered himself a birthday in the form of a transfer that changed his life. On the day he turned 22 the imposing Serbian striker signed for Juventus, as he had done four years earlier, leaving Partizan Belgrade – the club that had become too small for him – that same day. His destination was Tuscany and Fiorentina.

Before adopting Italy as his new lifestyle, the centre forward was stacking up the goals at school from the age of 10 in his native Serbia. The two big clubs of the country were not long in coming to learn about the phenomenon everyone had tried to attract. Red Star Belgrade pressed hard, but little Dušan finally opted for their rival: Partizan of Belgrade. At only 16 years and 22 days of age he made his debut in the Serbian league. Two months later he became the youngest to score a goal in the whole history of the club.

Dušan barely had time to make a name for himself in his own country before 'Fio' knocked on the door. The Viola poured just under €2 million into his signing, seeing Vlahović as the man to lead them out of their relative mire and restore the image of the club. Nicknamed the 'Batistuta of the 21st century' by the Viola fans in tribute to the prolific Argentinian, Dušan as the all-time top scorer of Fiorentina became a safe bet.

The attention of the big European clubs was becoming more and more pressing and Fiorentina were anxious to agree on a contract extension. It was a story of big money between a player ready to leave for free and a club keen to recover some sort of recompense in the event of a transfer. The Florentine president Rocco Commisso cried foul in the press, ensuring that Vlahović didn't walk away for nothing. Juventus got their man, but for a princely sum.

DID YOU KNOW?

Dušan Vlahović did not experience the war in Bosnia, but he was born there at the end of the conflict. Like many families in the former Yugoslavia, his own mourned the loss of a close member during those dark years: his older brother died during the armed conflict. As a tribute, Dušan got his brother's name tattooed on his right hand.

SPAIN

Nico

WILLIAMS

BORN: 12 July 2002, Pamplona, Spain

HEIGHT: 1.81 m

POSITION: Winger

PROFESSIONAL CAREER: CD Basconia, Athletic Bilbao B, Athletic Bilbao

DID YOU KNOW?

On 28 April 2021 in the famous San Mamés Stadium, match day 33 of La Liga, the substitutes at kick-off Iñaki and Nico Williams played side by side for the first time at the highest level of Spanish football. The match against Real Valladolid ended 2–2. This was the first time the Basque side had fielded two brothers in the same team since 1986, when Julio and Patxi Salinas tooled the field together for Athletic Bilbao.

It took just one match for Nico Williams to become the revelation of the 2024 European Championship in Germany. On 20 June in Gelsenkirchen, in the group stage, the Spanish Roja ripped apart the holders of the title, Italy. If the final scoreline was only 1–0, the result failed to fully emphasise the Spanish dominance. The Italians wilted in the face of the demonstration shown by the proud Iberians.

On the side of the central attacker, framing Álvaro Morata, the two young wingers Lamine Yamal on the right and especially Nico Williams on the left achieved outstanding performances. At 21, the recently internationally capped Basque adopted child had achieved the feat of seducing even fans of Barcelona and Real Madrid. It was a wonderful spotlight for the younger brother of Iñaki Williams, eight years his senior.

The Williams family is of Ghanaian origin, Nico's parents having travelled in extreme conditions to the Spanish enclave of Melilla. They were seeking political asylum and found refuge in Bilbao, where Iñaki was born. The family then moved to Pamplona before welcoming Nico eight years later. With the talent of the youngest and the success of the oldest, Athletic Bilbao was more than ready to sign Nicholas Williams Arthuer, whom everyone called 'Nico' in their training centre of Lezama.

With natural speed, innate dribbling and exceptional power the young winger quickly found himself in the first team, lining up against Real Valladolid in April 2021 in a match that ended in a 2–2 draw. Adept at rapid bursts of acceleration down the flank and of exact guided crosses, the young Basque brought additional offensive strength to the Athletic ranks.

On 23 November in Doha, replacing Marco Asensio against Costa Rica, the 20-year-old hopeful was given his FIFA World Cup bow. Nico had previously made his Spanish debut in September 2022 in a home defeat by Switzerland. While he featured in the game against Japan and the early exit against Morocco, two years later his star shone the brightest: in April 2024 the Williams brothers triumphed together in Seville, lifting the Spanish Cup after success in the final against RCD Mallorca. Euro 2024 in Germany saw Nico emerge as a star in his own right, excelling for the champions Spain as part of a thrilling attacking unit.

GERMANY

Florian

WIRTZ

BORN: 3 May 2003, Pulheim, Germany

HEIGHT: 1.77 m

POSITION: Attacking midfielder

PROFESSIONAL CAREER: Bayer 04 Leverkusen

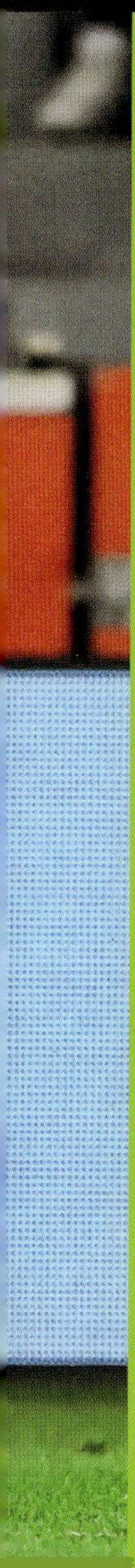

German prodigy Florian Wirtz is a young man in a hurry. It took him just seven seconds to surprise France, in March 2024 in Lyon, opening the scoring with a splendid strike in the international clash. Across the Rhine he holds plenty of firsts. A Bundesliga debut at just seventeen years of age for Bayer Leverkusen in a 4–1 win over Werder Bremen saw Wirtz become the youngest player since Yann Aurel Bisseck, in 2017 with FC Cologne, to start in the German top flight.

A month later Wirtz deceived Manuel Neuer for his first goal, and despite Bayern Munich winning the match 4–2 his success was still marked in the minds and notebooks of the statisticians as being the youngest goal scorer in Bundesliga history at 17 years and 34 days. This record was surpassed by Youssoufa Moukoko less than a year later, when aged 16 years and 28 days. Unsurprisingly, at the end of the season Wirtz was awarded the Fritz Walter Medal as the best youth player in the country.

The Wirtz star continued to ascend as he made his European bow by replacing the Argentinian Exequiel Palacios against Nice in the Europa League. Wirtz scored his first goal at this level shortly after, in a 6–2 demolition of the French team. A part of the German U-21 side that won the 2021 European Championship at that age group, there was little doubt Wirtz would one day play for the senior team.

A player who is energetic in style, the young prodigy covers a lot of ground throughout a game, sometimes popping up in midfield and sometimes on the left wing. Florian started at SV Grün-Weiß Brauweiler then joined the youth teams at FC Cologne from the age of eight. His potential was confirmed thereafter, and he subsequently joined Bayer Leverkusen in January 2020.

A torn cruciate ligament in the left knee in March 2022 could have interrupted the rapid ascent, but despite 10 months away Wirtz came back stronger both in his club and national teams. His first senior cap was earned in a 2–0 win over Liechtenstein. He missed the FIFA World Cup in Qatar but that turned into a blessing in disguise due to Germany's failure, eliminated in the group stages.

A sign of the influence of this outstanding talent was Wirtz's inspirational part in the sensational run of form by Bayer Leverkusen, winning the Bundesliga undefeated in 2024, prior to being a part of the German team in the European Championship they hosted that summer.

DID YOU KNOW?

To prepare for his baccalaureate in 2021, Florian Wirtz did not hesitate to miss a Europa League match against Slavia Prague before his exams. 'I know I have to approach my studies and football with the same energy,' he said. 'I can't give up so close to the end.' The choice was approved by his big sister Juliane, who plays for Werder Bremen.

SPAIN

Lamine

YAMAL

BORN: 13 July 2007, Esplugues de Llobregat, Spain

HEIGHT: 1.8 m

POSITION: Winger

PROFESSIONAL CAREER: FC Barcelona B, FC Barcelona

Talk about a rapid rise: Barcelona coach Xavi unleashed Lamine Yamal on an unsuspecting public in April 2023, the youngster making his debut for the Barcelona first team on 29 April, replacing Gavi in the 83rd minute of a 4–0 victory against Real Betis at 15 years, 9 months and 16 days of age. In August 2023, at the age of 16 years and 38 days, Yamal made his first full start in the famous colours and was crowned a Spanish champion at the year's end.

The young man's vision of the game is akin to a far more mature player and is incredible for his tender years. Capable of distributing silky passes, his speed and execution stunned onlookers from an early age. The quality of dribbles, even in exceedingly small areas of space, delights the fans and his vision for goal makes him an obvious threat. To top it off, his versatility on the ground is a huge plus for a coach in terms of tactics.

The teenager has been breaking all sorts of records since bursting onto the scene as a precocious youth. In 2012 the kid moved to Mató. He impressed his coach at CF Rocafonda and from the age of seven was redirected to La Masia, a true factory of champions, where he flourished from the outset. Six months after replacing Gavi in his debut match Yamal was enshrined as the league's youngest scorer, netting in a match against Granada that ended 2–2.

Yamal became the youngest player to participate in the Barca-Real Clasico, eclipsing a record that had stood since 1941 with a certain Vicente Martinez. In September 2023 Lamine Yamal celebrated his first selection with Spain, replacing Dani Olmo in the 44th minute in a Euro 2024 qualification match against Georgia when he was just 16 years and 57 days of age. He even scored the seventh goal of the 7–1 victory with his left foot, thus dethroning Gavi by becoming Spain's youngest scorer.

Still the accolades flowed. A remarkable Euro 2024 in Germany ended with a goal for the ages against France, a winner's medal around his neck and the Young Player of the Tournament Award. The sky is the limit for Lamine Yamal.

DID YOU KNOW?

On 21 April 2024 the Clasico between Real Madrid and FC Barcelona was one of the most controversial played. While the two teams were tied in the first-half at 1–1 Lamine Yamal seemed to score a goal, cleared off the line by Real goalkeeper Andriy Lunin. Images appeared to indicate that the ball had crossed the line, but the goal was not awarded. After Barça's 2–4 defeat and the numerous other controversies linked to this famous match, the Catalan leaders even considered appealing to the courts to have the match cancelled and replayed!

FRANCE

Warren

ZAÏRE-EMERY

BORN: 8 March 2006, Montreuil, France

HEIGHT: 1.78 m

POSITION: Midfielder

PROFESSIONAL CAREER: Paris Saint-Germain FC

DID YOU KNOW?

Having learned to play on a field in Marcel Cachin, little Warren, at the age of eight, couldn't get enough of football and even then had a history of challenging those bigger than him. One day he decided to join in at the municipal stadium of Romainville, leading his father on a merry chase around the city to find the runaway. 'When I found him I couldn't argue with him . . . even though I told his mother the opposite!' his father commented.

Replacing Marco Verratti in the 82nd minute at Gabriel Montpied Stadium on 6 August 2022 during PSG's 5–0 win over Clermont, Warren Zaïre-Emery's entire universe changed. At the age of 16 years, 4 months and 29 days he became the youngest player in the history of the club from the capital.

Making these statement moments is obviously in the genes of the native of Montreuil, since in November 2023 he became, at the age of 17 and 255 days, the youngest international to play in the France senior team since Maurice Gastiger, who set his mark back in 1914. The match, against Gibraltar in Nice, ended in a record 14–0 humbling of the minnows and 'Wawa', as he is affectionately known, even netted his first international goal.

Incredibly mature, this novice without an ego remained a calm squad member and his lucidity was a boon for the PSG collective. HIs performances owed much to his anticipation, followed by laser interventions of incredible cleanliness. An ability to recover a ball when lost and his energetic running are delights to watch, and pressure is an alien concept to him.

Zaïre-Emery started his football journey at FCM Aubervilliers, having a ball at his foot from the age of four and a half. Spotted by PSG, he integrated into the club's pre-training in 2014 and from his first appearance in the top team it was clear that Zaïre-Emery was exemplary. In March 2022, with Wawa barely out of his teens, PSG's then coach, Mauricio Pochettino, was taken by his ability and included him in the first-team set-up.

Four months later Zaïre-Emery signed his first professional contract, which initially bound him to Paris until 2025. Europe began to discover the new gem, and in an October 2023 UEFA Champions League fixture against AC Milan (a 3–0 win) the number 33 was elected man of the match. He subsequently became the youngest French scorer in the competition history when he equalised against Borussia in Dortmund at just 17 years and 280 days of age.

It was clear PSG wanted to keep Zaïre-Emery for quite some time, and they extended his contract until 2029. Having represented France at U-16s, U-17s, U-18s, U-19s and U-21s, an extended run in the senior team seems inevitable. In May 2024, without any hesitation, Didier Deschamps registered Wawa in his list of 25 players selected for the European championships in Germany.

Photographic credits

pp. ii–iii: Sergio Ruiz/Pressinphoto/Icon Sport; p. vi: Manuel Blondeau/Icon Sport; p. 2: Shutterstock; p. 4: Mark Cosgrove/News Images/Sipa USA/Icon Sport; JC Ruiz/Sipa USA/Icon Sport; p. 6: Thomas Bachun/Gepa/Icon Sport; Cesar Cebolla/Pressinphoto/Icon Sport; p. 8: Spi/Icon Sport; PA Images/Icon Sport; p. 10: Sportidia/Icon Sport; Anthony Dibon/Icon Sport; p. 12: Maurice van Steen/VI Images/Presse Sports; Petter Arvidson/Bildbyran/Icon Sport; p. 14: ANP/Icon Sport; Manuel Reino/DeFodi Images; p. 16: Maurice van Steen/VI Images/Presse Sports; Enrique de la Fuente/Shot For Press/Icon Sport; p. 18: Bagu Blanco/Pressinphoto/Icon Sport; LiveMedia/Icon Sport; p. 20: Icon Sport; Anthony Dibon/Icon Sport; p. 22: Anthony Bibard/FEP/Icon Sport; GSI/Icon Sport; p. 24: La Presse/Icon Sport; Robert Michael/dpa/PictureAlliance/Icon Sport; p. 26: Pierre Lahalle/Presse Sports; Bernd Feil/Mis/Icon Sport; p. 28: Vincent Van Doornick/Isosport/Presse Sports; Maksim Bogodvid/Sputnik/Icon Sport; p. 30: Gerrit van Keulen/VI Images/Presse Sports; Martin Rickett/PA Images/Icon Sport; p. 32: Maurice van Steen/VI Images/Presse Sports; p. 34: Maurice van Steen/VI Images/Presse Sports; p. 36: ANP/Icon Sport; zumapress.com/Avalon Photo by Icon Sport; p. 38: PA Images/Icon Sport; Spi/Icon Sport; p. 40: Sergio Ruiz/Pressinphoto/Icon Sport; Baptiste Fernandez/Icon Sport; p. 42: La Presse/Icon Sport; Marc Aspland/The Times/News Licensing/ABACAPRESS.COM/Icon Sport; p. 44: Christophe Saidi/FEP/Icon Sport; David Klein/Sportimage/Icon Sport; p. 46: Bagu Blanco/Pressinphoto/Icon Sport; NicolòxCampox/Imago/Icon Sport; p. 48: Massimo Rana/IPP/Presse Sports; Action Plus/Icon Sport; p. 50: Icon Sport; Actionplus/Icon Sport; p. 52: SUSA/Icon Sport; Marca/Icon Sport; p. 54: pi/Icon Sport; p. 56: PA Images/Icon Sport; p. 58: PA Images/Icon Sport; p. 60: Bagu Blanco/Pressinphoto/Icon Sport; Joan Gosa/Xinhua/Icon Sport; p. 62: Francesco Scaccianoce/LiveMedia/Sipa USA/Icon sport/Philippe Lecoeur/FEP/Icon Sport; p. 64: Spi/Icon Sport; Mis/Icon Sport; p. 66: ActionPlus/Icon Sport; PA Images/Icon Sport; p. 68: Pierre Lahalle/Presse Sports; Sandra Ruhaut/Icon Sport; p. 70: PA Images Icon Sport/Orange Creek/Icon Sport; p. 72: Carlos Silva/Icon Sport; p. 74: PA Images/Icon Sport; Vegard Grøtt/Bildbyran/Icon Sport; p. 76: PA Images/Icon Sport; p. 78: PA Images/Icon Sport; p. 80: Marcel/Firo/Icon Sport; Pierre Lahalle/Presse Sports; p. 82: Nicolò Campo/USA/Icon Sport; Hugo Pfeiffer/Icon Sport; p. 84: Alamy; Paul Harding/Getty Images; p. 86: Maurice van Steen/VI Images/Presse Sports; Actionplus/Icon Sport; p. 88: Tom Bode/Orange Creek/Icon Sport; Susa Icon Sport: p. 90: Joaquin Corchero Arcos/Cordon/Presse Sports; Harry Langer/DeFodi Images/Icon Sport; p. 92: dam Davy/PA Images/Icon Sport; Thorsten Wagner/Witters/Presse Sports; p. 94: PictureAlliance/Icon Sport; p. 96: Gerrit van Keulen/VI Images/Presse Sports; Jerome Prevost/Presse Sports; p. 98: Anthony Dibon/Icon Sport; Michael P Ryan/Sportsfile/Icon Sport; p. 100: Baptiste Fernandez/Icon Sport; Andrew Yates/Spi/Icon Sport; p. 102: Hugo Pfeiffer/Icon Sport; La Presse/Icon Sport; p. 104: Spi/Icon Sport/La Presse/Icon Sport; p. 106: Lisa Guglielmi/LiveMedia/DeFodi/Icon Sport; PA Images/Icon Sport; p. 108: Tomasz Jastrzebowski/Foto Olimpik/Presse Sports; Mis/Icon Sport; p. 110: Ulrik Pedersen/DeFodi Images/Icon Sport; Ulrik Pedersen/DeFodi Images/Icon Sport; p. 112: Newspix/Icon Sport; La Presse/Icon Sport; p. 114: Thiago Ribeiro/AGIF/Presse Sports; Michel Vincent/Presse Sports; p. 116: Baptiste Fernandez/Icon Sport; Hugo Pfeiffer/Icon Sport; p. 118: La Presse/Icon Sport; Spi/Icon Sport; p. 120: Dave Winter/Icon Sport; Manuel Blondeau/Icon Sport; p. 122: Icon Sport; p. 124: Maurice van Steen/VI Images/Presse Sports; Anthony Dibon/Icon Sport; p. 126: Bagu Blanco/Pressinphoto/Icon Sport; Tom Weller/dpa/Icon Sport; p. 128: Tom Weller/Eibner/Expa/Presse Sports; Thorsten Wagner/Witters/Presse Sports; p. 130: Gerrit van Keulen/VI Images/Presse Sports; Anthony Dibon/Icon Sport; p. 132: Hugo Pfeiffer/Icon Sport; p. 134: Anthony Dibon/Icon Sport; PA Images/Icon Sport; p. 136: PictureAlliance/Icon Sport; p. 138: Sergio Ruiz/Pressinphoto/Icon Sport; Antonio Pozo/Pressinphoto/Icon Sport; p. 140: Ulrik Pedersen/DeFodi/Icon Sport; Matteo Ciambelli/DeFodi Images/Icon Sport; p. 142: PA Images/Icon Sport; p. 144: Pressinphoto/Icon Sport; Baptiste Fernandez/Icon Sport; p. 146: PA Images/Icon Sport; De Fodi Images/Icon Sport; p. 148: Xavi Bonilla/DeFodi Images/Icon Sport; PictureAlliance/Icon Sport; p. 150: Simon Stacpoole/Offside/Presse Sports; PA Images/Icon Sport; p. 152: PA Images/Icon Sport; Vince Mignott/DeFodi Images/Icon Sport; p. 154: Paul Terry/Spi/Icon Sport; PA Images/Icon Sport; p. 156: Bagu Blanco/Pressinphoto/Icon Sport; Marca/Icon Sport; p. 158: Paul Chesterton/Expa/Presse Sports; Abaca/Icon Sport; p. 160: Sergio Ruiz/Pressinphoto/Icon Sport; Alberto Gardin/SOPA Images/Sipa USA/Icon Sport; p. 162: Matt Wilkinson/MB Media/Icon Sport; PA Images/Icon Sport; p. 164: Maurice van Steen/VI Images/Presse Sports; Ian Hodgson/PA Images/Icon Sport; p. 166: Baptiste Fernandez/Icon Sport; Manu Reino/DeFodi Images/Icon Sport; p. 168: PictureAlliance/Icon Sport; Matt Wilkinson/Expa/Presse Sports; p. 170: Sergio Ruiz/Pressinphoto/Icon Sport; David Martins/SUSA/Icon Sport; p. 172: Maurice van Steen/VI Images/Presse Sports; Charlotte Wilson/Offside/Presse Sports; p. 174: ANP/Icon Sport; Icon Sport; p. 176: PictureAllance/Icon Sport; Spada/La Presse/Icon Sport; p. 178: Pressinphoto/Icon Sport; Antonio Pozo/Pressinphoto/Icon Sport; p. 180: Anthony Dibon/Icon Sport; PA Images/Icon Sport; p. 182: Anthony Bibard/FEP/Icon Sport; ANP/Maurice van Stone/Icon sport; p. 184: Orange Creek/Icon Sport; Icon Sport; p. 186: Maurice van Steen/VI Images/Presse Sports; Tom Bode Multimedia/VI Images/Presse Sports; p. 188: Hugo Pfeiffer/Icon Sport; p. 190: Gianluca Ricci/LiveMedia/SUSA/Icon Sport; La Presse/Icon Sport; p. 192: Cesar Cebolla/Pressinphoto/Icon Sport; Sergio Ruiz/Pressinphoto/Icon Sport; p. 194: Federico Gambarini/dpa/Icon Sport; Gerrit van Cologne/ANP/Icon Sport; p. 196: Cesar Cebolla/Pressinphoto/Icon Sport; Sergio Ruiz/Pressinphoto/Icon Sport; p. 198: Anthony Dibon/Icon Sport; Philippe Lecoeur/FEP/Icon Sport; p. 201: Manuel Reino/DeFodi Images (top); ANP/Maurice van Stone/Icon Sport (bottom).

LEAGUE

4